Win!

Win!

Malcolm Macdonald

 Pelham Books · London

First published in Great Britain by
Pelham Books Ltd
52 Bedford Square London WC1B 3EF
1977

ISBN 0 7207 1014 6

Filmset in 10 point Century Schoolbook by
Saildean Phototypesetting Limited

Printed and bound in Great Britain by
Billing & Sons, Guildford, London and Worcester

Contents

Illustrations

Between pages 80 and 81

The author and publisher are grateful to the following for their kind
permission to reproduce the illustrations: to the Press Association Limited
for pictures 4, 5, 7 and 12; to Sporting Pictures (UK) Limited for 8, 10 and 11;
to Syndication International for 9; to Bill Smith for 13; and to the *Daily
Mirror* and photographer Monte Fresco for 14–17.

Acknowledgment

I should like to express my thanks to Tony Roche for his invaluable help with this book.   *Malcolm Macdonald*

The Name of the Game

So you want to be a pro. You believe you possess the ability, the determination and the character to go all the way to the top in professional football. Well I admire your confidence ... and between now and the last word in this book I am going to test that confidence to the limit.

There is no easy way into professional football. There are countless pitfalls, a lot of hard, honest, slogging years to overcome and setbacks capable of shattering the most concrete personality. On the other hand, life as a professional footballer is immensely rewarding, exciting and fulfilling – just as long as you appreciate that without work and dedication there can be no reward, only failure.

I do not know the extent of your ability, your physical capabilities or even which foot you prefer. Yet I do know that recurring dream you are having about being a pro.

But have you looked beyond the glory of playing in front of cheering crowds, the bright lights of life as a celebrity, the heady champagne years of television appearances, radio interviews and newspaper headlines?

I want you to forget all the trimmings. Let's get down to reality, to basics. The name of the game is 'earning a living'. You want to become a professional footballer. Therefore you are prepared to dedicate the best years of your life to a sport which can be demanding, cruel, instant in its rewards for success and hurtful in its rejection of failure.

A cynical outlook? No, just a realistic view of a game which ceases to be anything like the game you have played and do play outside the sphere of professionalism. Once you add the prefix 'professional', football becomes part and parcel of a different world.

There can be no half measures. You cannot tinker with becoming a pro in a half-hearted fashion. From the moment you get a toe-nail inside a club, you must work and work hard to persuade that club that they will be making a costly mistake if they let you go at the end of your apprenticeship.

But now I am jumping ahead. Let's go back to the first steps which you must take on the road to success. I want you to sit down and have a good old conversation with yourself. Ask if you are prepared to gamble on a career that could lie in ruins after two years. Ask if you really appreciate that you will not just be playing in a glamorous game, but actually earning your daily bread, for yourself and your future family.

If you are satisfied with the answers, and equally satisfied that you have been totally honest with yourself, then by all means go ahead. I am only too happy to give you all the advice and help possible. But do not be a fool to yourself at the outset.

By that I mean do not decide to enter professional football with the half-cocked idea that you will be happy to become a professional even if it means playing down in the lower divisions. You must set your sights at becoming the best in the business. Then, if it proves unavoidable, work backwards until you have found your level, work hard at that level, and begin working towards climbing back up.

In other words, never, never be satisfied with your lot in life. If you reach a certain level and decide that is where you are safe and secure, you will eventually slip backwards.

Just about now you are probably wishing you had not picked up this book in the first place. Well, if you give up now, you will never become a professional - and that is a promise.

The following chapters roughly chart my life as a professional footballer. But this is not an autobiography. I draw on certain experiences and use them as examples for your benefit. I go all the way back to my schooldays to illustrate the lack of basic understanding that exists at that level when it comes to young footballers.

As I move along, I will hammer advice in 'dos' and 'don'ts'. It is up to you whether or not you accept my advice. But remember, I offer it not out of a desire to hear my own voice or read my own words. I have been through what you are going to go through. If you want a helping hand along the road, keep reading.

I'll introduce you to some of the incredible characters I have encountered on my travels, some charming and others not so charming. You will meet them all. What matters is that you know how to handle them.

I'll advise you on how to look after your body, how to cope with diet problems, how to handle publicity - good and bad - and what to do during your vital years as an apprentice.

The word 'professional' is all-important. I have not neglected this. But be prepared for a few surprises when you come to chapter 4. Because there are two sides to being a professional and a lot that you must learn before you take one step in the direction of professionalism.

If there is one aspect of life as a professional footballer that I have missed, then I would like to know about it. And if you believe that I have by-passed something important, do not hesitate to question that omission.

Having thrown just about every obstacle in your way, I would like to add that nothing would give me more pleasure than to believe that I have helped a boy to make the grade. I know that there are countless youngsters kicking a ball around some park, garden or school-yard who will never enter professional football because (a) they never get the opportunity, and (b) they do not know enough about it. These youngsters are lost to the game at a time when there is so much waffle about the lack of talent coming through in English football and how far behind we have fallen in the way of skills and flair.

The talent is there. But where we do fall down is when it comes to·unearthing, dusting down, grooming and educating that talent. There are too many cobwebs in the thinking department of modern football. I want to see them cleared away and positive action taken to ensure that we no longer waste the wealth of talent currently buried under layers of ignorance at all levels, from school football upwards.

But do not become big-headed as you read these words. You have proved exactly nothing yet. You have it all to do. I sincerely hope that by the time you have finished this book, you will be someways better equipped to tackle the problems of becoming a professional footballer.

I want you to close the book after the last word and still be able to say, loudly, 'Yes, I want to be a pro.'

ONE

A Time for Play

The formative years

Mr Griffin scratched his head. I was not too sure whether my attempt at making a coffee table was driving him to distraction or whether Saturday's team-selection had him in a tizz. He scribbled down a list of names. My coffee table was not the problem.

'Who do we have to play in goal?' he said, tapping his pencil on the unplaned edges of my woodwork masterpiece. 'Who impressed in the pre-season trial games?'

We had a problem. Normally, goalkeeping is the weakest position in the first year at secondary school.

Suddenly, Mr Griffin jumped up off his stool. My coffee table clattered to the floor. 'I know', he said, 'I'll pick the school cricket-team wicket-keeper!'

Struggling to conceal my surprise, I ventured to question the logic behind so sudden a master-stroke.

'Use your common sense, lad,' he snapped. 'He's used to catching a ball, isn't he?'

There ended my first lesson in the art of team selection. Mr Griffin's logic was so simple as to be devastating. It was also an insight into the well-meaning mind of the school coach.

I was never too keen on woodwork. But Friday woodwork classes at Sloane Grammar School were something special when I was twelve. Mr Griffin, our woodwork master, was also in charge of the first-year football and cricket teams. On Fridays, with my delighted assistance, he selected the team for Saturday's match.

I doubt if that coffee table was ever finished. One nail a

15

week was the average extent of my labours. Mr Griffin usually guided the table out of my grasp after about ten minutes and began talking football tactics, who should play where and why – all the time applying the plane to a rough edge.

I was captain of the first-year team, and no mean player. But then, as is often the way, one young lad shows he can play better than the rest, and it is a case of: 'Stick him at centre-half, and build the rest of the team around him.'

Thank God I was not a very small boy with fragile bones. Not that I was particularly well-built when I was at school. I was average to small and not very heavy. My legs were the same shape as they are now – thinner – but the same shape.

Looking back on those fabulous years, I can see all the initial problems you face as a schoolboy. We are accepting that you are a good little footballer – way above average in your ability on the ball, and very promising as a young thinker. You are probably the boy to whom the others pass. You are the player they rely upon to pull off the master-stroke when they are losing. Your name is one of the first to go down on the team-sheet. But dangers lurk at every turn. Your career can be made or broken during these formative years, because these are the years in which you must develop your skills and develop your character.

To hell with coaching manuals. Out of the window with detailed tactics. Give a boy a football, point to a pitch, stick a number on his back and tell him: 'Go out and play. Enjoy yourself. Show us what you can do.' This is the message to yell from the rooftops. Because this is the all-important period in your life when you must fall in love with that ball. You must dribble with it, juggle with it, head it, fall over it and carry that ball off the pitch under your arm.

At no time should you be separated from the ball as long as you want the ball at your feet or in your hands. Never mind boring the pants off boys with 4-3-3, overlaps and diagonal runs.

Our games lessons followed a regular, frustrating pattern. We ripped off our clothes and laced up our boots in record time. Then we clawed at the dressing-room door to get out on the pitch. Everyone chatted and argued at once. One lad wanted to be Bobby Charlton, another insisted on being Johnny Haynes. We all wanted to play football and imitate our idols. Every week we hoped for a reprieve. But every week we spent almost half our allotted time listening to waffle.

Our games master would swagger out, new blue tracksuit dotted with badges, a whistle around his neck and the ball under one arm. 'Gather round me, boys,' were the words we feared. We grudgingly formed the eternal circle as he droned on and on about tactics, who should be covering whom, where to draw our lines of confrontation, what to do at set-pieces. All we wanted to do was play football.

We had numbers on our backs. That is sufficient organisation for lads of twelve and thirteen. If a youngster wears the number five shirt, he knows he is playing centre-half. Give the lad a number eleven shirt and he knows where to find the left wing. What more does any lad of that age need to know about the game he loves?

Precious minutes of our football period ticked away as our master waved his free arm in mysterious arcs that encompassed us and the pitch. His other arm kept a firm grip on the ball. Deep down he knew that we were all watching that ball, waiting for the moment when he relaxed his grip.

So what happened to his tactics? The same thing that always happens with lads of that tender age. We kicked our boots into the ground, fidgeted, quietly groaned and agonised over his shining wrist-watch which confirmed that our maths lesson was drawing closer by the minute. When we finally escaped, little if any of our master's tactical lecture was ever mirrored in our play. The lads who could play played; those who couldn't chased the ball in a furious herd.

Perhaps some of those less talented boys were late developers. But I doubt it. Even at twelve and thirteen, you know which of your class-mates you prefer to have on your side. And when teams are picked in the playground, the same handful of lads are always the last to be picked.

Our master had good intentions. He was doing his best for

17

his pupils. But he was also secretly enjoying a little ego trip, showing off his limited football knowledge to minds that were far too young to grasp what he was talking about. For all we knew, our master might have just bought the latest coaching book at W.H. Smith's bookshop around the corner, skipped through the chapters until he found a subject that took his fancy, and lectured us on some aspect of play, totally out of context. The trouble was and is, such lectures certainly sound convincing.

You will experience the same kind of situation. You will ache to get on with playing as the words drift over your head. It is so very important that you should have the freedom to let your natural skills emerge, unhindered and unaffected by dangerous, albeit well-intentioned, instructions and advice from men who are simply not qualified to educate young footballers. Only when you have found your football feet – and know what those feet can do – will you be ready to learn about the game at a technical level.

Take on and beat six opponents in the school-team. The experience will prove invaluable. Your reflexes will sharpen, your balance and timing will improve. Your vision will widen, your skills will develop. They have to. Otherwise, with scores of boys all chasing the same ball, you will rarely get a touch of it or forever be caught in possession.

What astonishes me is the naive attitude of some games masters. I began as a centre-half. An average physique but more than average ability earmarked me as the automatic choice for the pivot's role and the job of team stalwart. There is, of course, what to a school-teacher is a logical reason for selecting players on such a basis. A teacher must look at the situation from every angle. He is responsible for the safety of his pupils as well as their sporting development. Hardly surprising, then, that most teachers would rather shove a skinny, bespectacled youngster out on a wing rather than be responsible for his risking life and limb in a more central part of the pitch where tackles are strong and challenges regular. Yet Denis Law was a frightening assortment of thin limbs, few ounces and glasses when he was a schoolboy. I wonder

18

where Denis was shoved before his natural genius battled through.

Going back to Mr Griffin's team-selection – that lad who ended up in goal because he was a wicket-keeper later developed into a good left-winger in the fourth year. Another boy who rarely got a game because he always believed he was a forward ended up playing in goal at senior amateur level when he was twenty.

By the time I was thirteen, I was selected to play for the senior team. They were seventeen and eighteen-year-olds and physically bigger than me. So I was shunted out to the proverbial left-wing. We won, I scored one goal and laid on the other two.

The next day, I took the master by surprise when I asked: 'Where are you playing me next week?' It had not occurred to me either that I might have been returned to the second-team or that I might have been dropped to make way for the senior player whose place I originally filled. The master gave me an old-fashioned look. When I didn't even blink, he spluttered: 'Hm, er ... inside-left.'

I was not trying to be smart, nor was I suffering from a swelled head. I simply believed that I was good enough for the senior team, and that I had merited another game. My character was beginning to emerge.

At fifteen, I filled out a bit and was moved to centre-forward. But I still believe that my size and age mattered as much, if not more, than how I was playing.

I was a niggler when I wore that number nine shirt. Opposing centre-halves who were used to playing against the average school forward – big but limited – were never too sure how to handle a little lad of fifteen who competed more strongly than the rest.

How many lads take one look at the size of an opponent and decide that they do not fancy the next ninety minutes? When they come off the park they know their contribution has done little to help the cause. Heart and character never materialised because the ready-made excuses were there before the kick-off. I had a mean streak which came out whenever I pulled on a striker's shirt. Size never mattered. I wanted to score goals, wanted to be the best in the team. That attitude helped my character to emerge – yet it was my character that produced my attitude. Sounds a contradiction. But think about it. Heart and character go together.

I expect every games master reading this chapter is on the verge of writing me blood-red letters of protest. Gentlemen, hold those pens for a few more paragraphs. I want to establish the importance of teachers knowing how to help young players. I am not out to just decry their efforts. This is not a knocking session at the efforts of well-intentioned professional men. Without proper guidance, however, and I stress the word 'proper', your career will flounder on the first step of the ladder.

I was fortunate to have a teacher such as Mr Griffin when I was twelve. He always tempered his more extraordinary ideas by saying: 'I only know enough about football to select the first-year team. Therefore I will only attempt to answer football questions at that level.'

For an adult to make such an admission to schoolboys required a lot of moral courage. Yet we loved him for it. He commanded our respect more than would have a bluffer.

Mr Griffin encouraged us to ask questions. But when we went above his head with a real puzzler, he would wave a finger and say: 'That's a naughty one, lad. I'm not going to guess, nor am I prepared to attempt an answer based on my limited knowledge at that level.'

Because of his honesty and character, we were never afraid to ask questions. We did not attempt to catch him out. Mr Griffin meant too much to our football team and we loved him because he never tried to put us down with blustering, detailed answers, geared to go over our heads and to disguise a lack of knowledge.

Not for one moment am I suggesting that schoolboys of twelve and thirteen are capable of thought and appreciation of character at such depth. But I do know that we respected that man. Only later, as we grew up, did we fully understand why.

How many young footballers are afraid of asking a question because they are afraid of being made to look foolish? Thousands! Are you afraid of asking about what you do not know or understand? I was. Often, there is good reason for such fears.

I remember a teacher who attended a coaching seminar some years ago. He had no coaching qualifications, but he went with a number of PE masters to see how seminars are run. One afternoon, some of the visiting teachers sat in on a lecture by a well-known First Division manager. What the manager discussed is neither here nor there. But already, the games master in question was soaking up the atmosphere. There he sat, tracksuit spotless and new, among known professional coaches, and loving every minute of the experience. He left that seminar with a fragment of unrelated knowledge in his head. He had not heard the previous day's lecture, nor would he hear the following day's lecture. As far as he was concerned, however, he had heard more than enough to cover the next few weeks' sports periods.

I can picture the scene the day he faced his pupils for the first sports period after his return. Those lads took an incredible ear-bashing about tactics. Not one of them, however, had the confidence to question anything he was being told.

I made the same mistake. I stood and listened to utter garbage - not that I knew that for a fact - but even at twelve my scraped-up football knowledge, mostly acquired on the Fulham terraces, told me that what I was hearing was faulty. Yet I did not have the courage of my convictions to put up my hand and say: 'Excuse me, sir, but ...' My question might have been well received. But I was afraid of being shown up by some lengthy, technical reply that would have soared even higher over my lightly-filled head.

The games master who dashed back from that seminar to impress his pupils was also making the effort out of the best possible intentions. He wanted to pass on football tips which he believed would benefit them. It is this region of communication which worries me most of all - this region where good intentions, and a little learning being a highly dangerous thing, are two elements harmful to you. Nobody will deliberately set out to spoil your chances. Yet there are hundreds of people who may do just that because they don't know any better.

Character formation is equally important. My headmaster summoned me one day and said: 'You have neglected your lessons because you are spending too much time thinking about football and playing football.'

I tried to argue, but he waved my protests aside and instructed the games master to relegate me to the second team. I flared up when I heard the news that I was dropped from the senior team. I could have stomached extra homework or detention. But this was brutal punishment as far as I was concerned. It was meant to be. The headmaster knew exactly how to shake me up.

I tried to make my games master see reason, but he, too, had his orders. In a final outburst I announced that unless I was picked for the senior team I wouldn't play at all. That got a reaction, but not in the way I had hoped. My games master looked up, stared me straight in the face and replied: 'If this is going to be your attitude, Macdonald, then I can only assume I was wrong about you, lad. You are nothing more than a big, overgrown baby.'

Having sunk in the knife, he resisted the temptation to turn the handle, choosing instead to withdraw the blade very gently: 'Don't stand there and tell me that you're refusing to play for the second team, lad. Go out tomorrow and play the game of your life. Make your point and your protest, but do it on the pitch.'

I remember thinking, 'I'll show the lot of them,' and I did. We won 6–0. I played well and felt a much better person after the whole incident. I was able to look the headmaster, my games master and my class-mates straight in the face. That is a lovely feeling.

Neither the headmaster nor the games master tried to form my character by their actions. They were using their wealth of experience in dealing with youngsters to *draw out* my character. They were prepared to help, but the basic responsibility was my own. At this level, school coaches have so much to offer, so much to contribute in the way of character formation.

Having said that, I emphasise the point – don't preach to youngsters at an age when they should be out playing football, loving every muddy minute. If you overdo the heavy tactical jargon, you risk turning boys against football altogether.

Do not take that statement lightly. I have seen it happen.

Take one twelve-year-old schoolboy. Give him a football kit and a ball. Select him in your team. Watch his excitement mount as kick-off time approaches. Now keep him hanging around in his kit while you expound lofty theories. I guarantee that before very long, that little boy grows to dislike games lessons and develops a none-too-sure attitude about football because he is baffled by all the trimmings. In the end, he will decide he dislikes football because it is boring.

Where the unqualified coach can help is by encouraging lads who lack confidence, and by slapping down those who grow too big for their size four boots. A boy who believes he is so good that he can play when he feels like playing needs a verbal boot up the backside. Tell him he cannot play. Tell him he is not as good as he thinks he is. Leave him out of the team ... and watch the reaction. As his character emerges, he will battle you, fight to prove you wrong. That is the reaction of a boy with a future. If, however, he continues to show no interest, resist the urge to thicken his ear and resist the urge to ignore him altogether.

Far be it from me to tell teachers how to do their job. But I am concerned with one aspect of their job that overlaps with mine. And I know that no teacher would appreciate it if I appeared in their science lab, and began lecturing on physics.

No, when that young lad ignores your initial attempts at bringing out his strong side, increase the volume of the verbals. Persist where there is ability. Who knows what may lie behind his attitude?

I have a fear that many good youngsters are lost to football

23

because somewhere along the line they were badly in need of professional advice and finished up with a head full of waffle, bigger problems and a growing dislike for a game they once loved.

Frustration can drive a young boy away from the thing he loves most of all. The frustration of wanting to play the game when his head is being crammed with facts and figures. Followed by the frustration of being at odds with those tactics when he is older because he never had the opportunity to develop his skills in the first place.

I have mentioned school coaches countless times in this chapter. I doubt if I have enlarged my circle of friends. But I mean no disrespect to you as professionals. I just plead with you all to think and think again before you hold your next football lesson.

The same principles that I have established throughout this chapter, and indeed this book, relate just as much to Scout coaches, youth club coaches, park football coaches ... all the men who have the opportunity of working with young footballers. Young lads need you, gentlemen, they need you one and all. But allow them the right to develop naturally. Do not complicate what is so simple and beautiful a game. Believe me, there are sufficient people waiting to do just that when they grow up.

TWO

The Apprentice

Your reputation as a footballer quickly spreads beyond the confines of the school walls. Your class-mates are quick to appreciate that you have a special talent. Total strangers, who watch you play for your school team, pass the word: 'That young lad, what's-his-name, he's different class.'

Before very long, League club scouts take an interest. By the time you are fifteen a number of League clubs are definitely interested. And your parents get used to hearing knocks on their door at unexpected hours as the scouts make their initial approaches. The scouts want you to sign apprentice professional forms for their club. But they realise that you can sign nothing without the consent of your parents. Nor can you put pen to paper until you are sixteen and legally of school-leaving age.

Now you face one of the most difficult decisions of your whole life – a decision you must make at a very tender and impressionable age. So it is important that you know what to look for in your future employer.

The question you must ask is not: 'Shall I sign?' but more important: 'For whom shall I sign, and why?' Your whole football career lies in the balance as you consider the various offers, some from the big glamour clubs, and others from the smaller, less famous clubs.

The first mistake youngsters usually make is that they judge the clubs on the basis of size and reputation. Without proper guidance, you might think: 'Do I risk joining a big, famous club and hope that I become a star, or do I join a club from the lower divisions and become a big fish in a small pond?'

This outlook is totally wrong. You should make a point of going to watch each of the teams in action. You should make a note of how many young players, former club apprentices and juniors, are playing in the first team; how many lads have come all the way up through the club's youth system to make the grade as professionals.

Here is your gauge. Not fame and name. What matters is – how does each club treat its youngsters? Does it produce a fair percentage of first-team players from its own back yard – or does it rely heavily on big-money signings while its juniors drift away, disillusioned, to play in the lower divisions?

In too many clubs, managers and first-team coaches do not even know the names of their apprentice professionals. They take too little interest in their young players. Every once in a while, the youth team coach goes to see the manager about a young lad who is showing great promise. The lack of genuine enthusiasm that greets his announcement is enough to floor the man in the first place. Then he is told that he is doing a grand job and to carry on getting a few results in the Youth League.

So the youth team coach often has to generate his own enthusiasm and impart it to the youngsters in his charge. Once he begins to feel that there is a widening gap between his job and the jobs above him, the whole system begins to slide into decay.

Often the junior coach is new to his job, and is as concerned for his own future as the futures of his players, if not more so.

It is a worrying fact that too few managers bother to watch their apprentice professionals in action regularly. Yet the youngsters are the life-blood of every club. They need advice, encouragement and the security of knowing that the man at the top is interested in their progress.

You must accept, before you take your first big step, that an apprenticeship in professional football can be the most heartbreaking experience a young man can have. You must not go into football with your head full of the bright lights, the big headlines, fame, fortune and glory. You must be prepared for the disappointment of spending two whole years of your youth learning about professional football, only to be discarded, told you are not wanted, possibly even told, 'Sorry, son, you won't make it. You just can't play.'

This is the other side of the game – the side too few young lads know about when that scout knocks on their door and widens their eyes with talk of 'Melchester Rovers', a professional career and all the attractive trappings of big football.

If you are aware of the pitfalls, the heartbreaks and the dangers of being starry-eyed, you have a far better chance of making a success of your apprenticeship. Because you will always be aware of the reality of failure. Should the worst come to the worst and you have to stomach lack of success you will still feel bitter disappointment. But you will not be totally shattered and incapable of putting the pieces back together.

Too many failed apprentices leave football feeling bitter towards the game for the rest of their lives. I want to ensure that you go into football with both eyes open and properly armed to cope with all eventualities.

I emphasise this discouraging aspect of apprentice professionalism for one reason: very few apprentices make the grade. This is a sad but very true fact. What is so shocking is the additional fact that the failure rate is high because many clubs do not take sufficient interest in their young players.

Sometimes there is no alternative open to a club. They know that for the benefit of the young player's future, they must tell him the painful truth. He is a good player. But not good enough to make it in the professional game. However, too many good youngsters are lost to football, not because they fail to respond to coaching, not because they lack the ability, but because they are neglected during the formative part of their football careers.

When I say 'clubs', I am not tarring every club with the same brush. There are extremely good ones where young players receive excellent guidance, encouragement and the necessary grounding. These are the clubs which prefer to concentrate on their youth policy. They maintain a high rate of activity at the grass-roots level, grooming young lads to play in their first team rather than gamble and hustle through the transfer-system.

Some clubs opt for this policy through choice. They have good support, enough money to keep creditors off their door-step, and the knowledge that they can tap the transfer market if they want a particular player. These clubs, however, prefer to develop their youngsters as much as possible.

Other clubs – Burnley are a good example – have to adopt a strong, productive youth policy to survive. Their financial position does not allow them to sign big cheques whenever they want a player. Over the years, Burnley have produced countless international footballers off their remarkable youth team 'conveyor belt'. They have scouted for young players, brought them to Turf Moor, given them every possible assistance to become good professionals, then either kept them or sold them. But always there is another batch coming through at Burnley: a sure sign of a strong youth policy.

At the opposite end of the financial scale there is Arsenal who have the resources to maintain a wide and comprehensive scouting net. They have the pick of the young players coming through, both in Britain and Southern Ireland. They also have the money to buy players when they so desire. But the money they spend on scouting every year demands that they produce at least two 'successful' apprentices per season. By successful I mean good enough to play for Arsenal or good enough to attract offers from other clubs. The money received through such a transfer goes towards the expense of teaching these two youngsters their trade, and towards the cost of teaching those other young apprentices who failed to make the grade.

And so the wheel keeps turning. The system is kept well oiled, productive, and at times capable of unearthing a crock of gold.

But again there is a great deal you must learn before you make your decision. Without knowing it, you are in danger of becoming tangled up in the seedier, financial side of football. I wonder how many directors, managers and coaches view young players, not as worthwhile football material but as mobile pound notes? You must take your time, listen and learn – ask, where and when it is possible, for advice. You must seek and find a club where your future matters to them.

Such a club allows the apprentices to train with and work with the senior professionals at some stage of every week; it is where the seniors are not a selective group, separate from the rest of the players and the sole interest of the manager and coach who spend all their time working on and planning for the next match.

Winning the next match is important. It is vital. But also vital is the education of the young players, because they are the seniors of the future. Unless they are allowed to blend in with the seniors and learn from them, they fall behind in their football education. A big and worrying gap appears between the age and experience levels within the club.

When this is the situation and the manager comes to bring a young lad into the first team, he discovers that the lad is confused, overawed and lost not because he lacks ability but because he is playing in a team with virtual strangers. There is even the danger of the youngster being as nervous in the company of his new team mates as he is of the opposition!

If you join a club where there are players that you used to watch and idolise from the terraces, you will freeze when you are thrust into a team that contains those same former idols – unless you have grown to feel part of the whole club and been allowed to train alongside well-known players from the beginning of your apprenticeship.

Too much short-sightedness within football has led to the ruination of many young careers. Clubs must realise that to survive they must abandon this 'We must win tomorrow and to hell with all else' complex. Win tomorrow by all means. That is what the game is all about – winning. But winning must be in the long term, not an overnight sensation. How many teams have hit the headlines through winning a major honour and never been heard of again for years.

These are the teams of clubs which concentrated on the present without giving sufficient thought to the future. Had they bothered to pay more attention to the likes of you, the reader, they would still have won their major honour and then been able gradually to inject fresh blood into the team without losing their status. As their team aged, the benefits of allowing you to train with the seniors would be reaped.

You could step into the first team feeling part of the set-up, the natural successor to the professional stepping down. It is that age and experience gap, of which I spoke earlier, that dooms teams to spend years in the wilderness while their young players catch up. Good teams break up because there is a lack of integration within the club. The young players are not ready, and the transfer market has failed, time and again, to plug gaps in fading teams.

One of the problems clubs face is that of accommodating young players who join them as apprentices. A fair percentage of young lads come from Scotland, Ireland or the north of England to join say, Spurs or Arsenal. Northern clubs are faced with the same problem when lads come across the Irish Sea or up from London.

Usually, clubs put their young players into digs, where possible, with a motherly landlady. But this is not enough. The lonely young man needs the company of his own age group. This leads to all sorts of frustrations until the apprentice begins to drift into the wrong company just to *have* company.

I believe the time has come for clubs to think in terms of building hostels for their young players. Arsenal and Spurs 'share' North London. Their training grounds – London Colney and Cheshunt respectively – are both in Hertfordshire. What is to stop them from building a hostel to billet twenty or thirty lads? They could share the cost – which would work out far cheaper for both clubs – and the lads would have company, feel part of a young community and be able to discuss the game amongst themselves, always able to advise and learn from each other. A married couple could live in and look after the needs of the lads. This would not, then, be a substitute for home life, which digs always appear to be. No, they would immediately feel part of a new and professional set-up that also affords them companionship.

Off the field, the lads need to learn discipline, manners, how to live away from home – all very important aspects of the education a young person requires in any walk of life.

A club with such a hostel would be ideal for young apprentices. The hostel alone would be a good indication of how much the club cared for young players.

Having made up your mind and agreed to join the club of your choice, you enter the world of professional football for the first time. You are sixteen, keen, excited and a little nervous. But you are not naive – not if you have read this chapter. You know that what faces you is not going to be all roses. But you are going to have a marvellous time because you are now steeled for all shocks.

Depending on the traditions within your club, your duties will vary. You will have to train, listen, learn. Never forgetting to ask questions about aspects of the game that you do not understand. You will face other responsibilities, such as those character-forming jobs of work to be done in the changing rooms and around the ground.

I prefer to push the clock forward two years at this stage to rejoin you on the morning you are summoned to the manager's office to be told that you are not going to be retained. You have served your apprenticeship. You have done reasonably well. Whatever the reasons, however, your club are not prepared to offer you professional forms. You are told hopefully, in the nicest way possible, and emerge from the office either angry and red-faced or struggling to keep a tight lip and dry eyes.

Now is the moment of truth. Do you throw your boots into your bag and storm out of the main gates or do you sit down and think about your future? You must do the latter. Because rejection by one club does not mean the end of the road; sometimes it represents the opening of new doors and the beginning of a whole new career.

The danger is that your apparent failure to make the grade after two years with one club will leave you so hurt that you may consider hanging up your boots – at eighteen! But believe me, there are hundreds of professional footballers only too willing to testify that their 'failure' at one club became a success story with another club. However, a lot depends on the tenacity and determination of the young player. The tragedy is that so many young lads, who are rejected by their first club after two years as apprentices, throw in the towel. They waste two invaluable years of an education that so many of their age would dearly love to receive. Never throw away those years. Have confidence and faith in your ability. If someone slaps you down, spring back and tell them that you are going to prove them wrong – and enjoy doing it.

You only have to look at the incredible blunders made by leading clubs over the past fifty years to realise that nobody in football is infallible. Players who have won countless caps for their country and major domestic honours often look back to the early part of their career when they were told that they were too small, too thin, short-sighted, too one-footed or just sub-standard. Every season a few young players leave their club for the last time, not realising that in five years' time they are going to pull an England or Scotland shirt over their heads.

Earlier I said that very few apprentices make the grade. This is true. But perhaps if more of them dug their heels in and battled for recognition with another club, the percentage might improve.

You make your decision. You sit down and have a good think. You decide to fight for your career and make immediate plans to secure a position with another club. If you fail to get an opening, you must be prepared to go down a grade. For example, if your original club play in the First Division and you want to stay at that level but cannot, then you must be prepared to go down a division, or two or three!

32

Sometimes, by making a fresh start with a small, struggling club, a young player with courage and determination can make his name in spite of his club, and work his way back to the top. This happens all the time.

Perhaps, without knowing it, you are a late developer. You may require two or three years at a lower level to find your feet. You will still be able to make a reasonable living, without too much pressure, and work at your game until your strengths emerge. If your first club happen to play in the Fourth Division, there is still a lower level. There is always a lower level. You can learn a lot through spending a few years playing with a Northern or Southern League semi-professional club. I should know. I learned a hell of a lot with Tonbridge.

There, I was played at right-back, left-back, midfield and on the wings. By the time I came into League football, I knew what it entails to play in those positions. This is a very important part of any footballer's education.

If you are told to play in a variety of positions, you must accept the instruction, and appreciate the benefits. What better way is there of learning about the strengths and weaknesses of a position than by occupying it?

Having played as a defender, I know a lot more about the problems that defenders face than I would ever have learned had I always played as a forward. There is nothing quite like practical experience.

So, if you begin with Melchester Rovers, spend two years there as an apprentice and are told you are not going to make the grade, you must not allow yourself to become bitter. You can still enjoy your football, even if you have to leave the Football League to establish your niche. Once that niche is established you can grasp the healthy, challenging job of working your way back up the ladder.

So far, I have discussed what you will experience and what you must do in the event of your apprenticeship ending in failure. Obviously, the other, happier side of the story is where you complete your apprenticeship and are told that you are to be offered a contract.

This side of the story will be handled later, because there are two sides to every story and now is the time for you to learn about the alternatives open to you.

There are many alternatives. In fact you may never be offered an apprenticeship. You may carry on playing until your ability is spotted by a local amateur or semi-professional club. This is another, quite different, path to professional football as a career. When I joined Southern League Tonbridge, I discovered that, unlike the situation at many League clubs, where the young players rarely work with the seniors, I was always training with players of tremendous experience – men who had either played non-League football for years after brief spells with League clubs, or who had played League football for years and wanted to carry on playing when their League career began to wane.

So never turn up your nose at the prospect of beginning your football career outside the Football League. The experience factor is of paramount importance to your future. Don't underestimate the advantages of learning your trade in the company of players who, possibly, have experienced every level of football, every thrill and disappointment.

Don't be a wise-guy. Don't make poor jokes about the older players stiffening in the joints. They can offer you so much in terms of knowledge and advice. Listen, learn, be prepared to be put in your place. Never adopt the attitude that the man giving you advice is on the way down and therefore a has-been. Remember, even if he is a has-been, you are still a never-have-been and may be a never-will-be unless you buckle down to learning your trade.

One of the things that you will certainly learn from older, experienced players is that football is basically a very simple game, complicated by the people in it – coaches, managers and semi-educated 'experts'.

Now is the appropriate moment to introduce the key to your football future – hunger: You must be consumed with a hunger for success, a hunger to win. No matter what obstacles are put in your way, you must scale them and feed the hunger that drives you on to success. If that urge stays in your belly throughout your career, you and your eventual family will never want for food.

The way to satisfy the hunger for success is by doing things simply. Play football the way it should be played. Do the simple things well. Live a simple, uncomplicated life. The simplicity of your existence will allow you to keep your life and your career in perspective at all times.

When you are faced with the problems that will certainly confront you, the strength of a simple, uncomplicated approach to life will see you through. Whether the problems come on the field or off it, you will be in the correct frame of mind to cope. You won't be frightened, confused or swamped with complicated, conflicting theories and ideals.

What do I mean by 'simplicity'? Football is all about putting the ball in at one end and keeping it out at the other – surely that is simple enough for anybody to comprehend? If you think a little more deeply, you will discover, as I have, that life is pretty much the same ... progress in your career by going forward, never forgetting to keep a close watch on your established achievements. In other words, as you work your way into your football career, battling to be a winner, you must never forget what you have learnt just because you move from one playing level to another, higher level.

Apprenticeship is an exciting time in the life of a young footballer. It leads to success or failure. This must be accepted from the beginning. But the failure need not be total. It can be a stepping-stone to success elsewhere.

Perhaps you will enter football without completing an apprenticeship. But while you may not complete the standard two year apprenticeship with a professional club, whatever period of time you spend learning from other, more experienced players will constitute an apprenticeship just the same.

Every player must go through the apprenticeship stage, whether it happens to be with Melchester Rovers or non-League Plugaway Villa. Your apprenticeship will be the time you spend learning how to become a professional footballer.

THREE
The Professional

I have outlined the two best-known ways in which you can enter professional football – through an orthodox apprenticeship with a Football League club or being spotted by a scout and invited to play for a non-League club. I have also emphasised that both roads to the top are paved with problems. You may flounder, either through bad luck, injury or the fact that you are not up to professional standard. But having examined the situations that arise when your apprenticeship ends in disappointment, let us now take you on the road to success.

When I say 'success' I mean the initial success achieved when, after two years' apprenticeship, you are told: 'We want you to turn professional with this club.' You have 'made it' – or at least that is the way you feel as you walk out of the manager's office after hearing the words you have longed to hear. But your battles are only just beginning.

The very fact that you feel ten feet tall because you are wanted by your club is, in itself, a danger. Your elation, your desire to run down the road yelling the news to the world, your feeling of immense satisfaction and relief after months of worrying and wondering – these are blinkers that can restrict your mental attitude and impair your mental vision.

You must get this understandable excitement out of your system before you settle down to thinking about your new, professional status. Otherwise you may sign your name to a piece of paper – and regret it for the rest of your football career.

36

This is the most critical period in your football life. So often, the young footballer greets the news that he is to become a professional with a delight born of dreams of glory and fame, stardom and adulation. Few young players give enough thought to the bread-and-butter side of their futures.

It is all very well, and healthy, to dream of Wembley and of playing for England, Ireland, Scotland or Wales. But there are two sides to professionalism. I will deal with the business side, the bread-and-butter side, the hard-cash side, first. Only when you are properly educated about the economic side of your career will I begin to discuss the playing aspects of professionalism.

The first thing you must do to become a professional is to sign a professional contract. Let us establish one very important fact from the outset. The business of signing a contract is not just a matter of putting pen to paper in a gesture of gratitude to the club for accepting you as a professional. Contracts are all about business: business is all about considered thought, negotiation and common sense. When a football club offer you a contract, they are not doing you a favour. Nor are you doing the club a favour by signing. The club want the player, and it is up to the player to apply the simple law of economics: supply and demand.

When you sign your first contract, you will set your own standards for the rest of your football career. I want to ensure that you know exactly what you are signing, and for what, before you pick up that pen.

The danger lies in the attitude that so many young players adopt when confronted with their first contract. They sign with the secret conviction that everything will improve as their careers develop. But this rarely happens.

When I joined Fulham from Tonbridge, it meant that I doubled my travelling time every day. And because I had to travel to the ground three, and sometimes four, times a week more than when I was with Tonbridge, it meant that my travelling expenses multiplied by four! Yet when I examined the cold, hard figures, it turned out that I was earning just £5 a week more than I had earned as a part-timer with a

Southern League club. I was travelling over 60 miles a day, sometimes five and six times a week, and by the end of the season, I had just managed to scrape through financially.

My first season with a Football League club turned out to be a reasonable one from my point of view. But Fulham were relegated to the Third Division and, as a result, financial belts were pulled in a notch. Wage rises were very difficult to obtain, and my application for a £5 rise was refused.

So I was left with the choice of remaining with Fulham and clinging on, just below the bread-line level, or of asking for a transfer. The first alternative would have also meant long spells in the reserve team. The second, a transfer, always presents big difficulties. Do not assume that obtaining a transfer is simply a matter of dropping an envelope on your manager's desk.

Fortunately, a transfer came my way. I signed for Luton Town. And although they, too, were a Third Division club, my wages doubled. This was very fortunate indeed for me because I could have been left languishing in Fulham's Football Combination team, very hard-up and slowly growing sick and disillusioned of football.

This is why I insist that you look out for yourself from the beginning of your professional career. It is a mug's game to sign any old contract thrust under your immature nose with the half-hope that everything will turn up trumps in the end. I appreciate that the human element comes into things at this vital stage. Nobody enjoys asking for money. In fact the embarrassment that people experience, in all walks of life, when it comes to asking for money is the trump card in the hands of every employer.

There is nothing wrong with asking for what you believe you are worth. But here again, I understand how some lads feel. They cannot bring themselves to sit in front of their manager and say: 'But I am a very good player, and I am worth ...'

This embarrassment is something you must overcome, unless you want to be trampled on from the outset. You **must stand up for yourself from the beginning. Don't be** embarrassed. Don't allow the words to catch on the back of your throat. You must explain, in detail, what you want. Don't be afraid to outline the standard of living which you believe to be your right, and the right of your future family. Never forget the old saying: 'The highest penny you bid is the penny you bid for yourself.'

There are, of course, difficulties involved in signing contracts. There is a rule in the contract, set before every professional footballer, which states that no outside agent may negotiate with, or on behalf of, the footballer. The more you think about that clause, rule or whatever you might like to call it, the more you realise the full implications – and restrictions, as far as the player is concerned.

How easy it would be to allow an accountant to make the necessary demands on your behalf. There would be no embarrassment. The whole business could be completed in an atmosphere of mutual understanding. The procedure would come as no shock to the professional accountant. He would act under direct instruction from his client – you – who would be spared the ordeal by pen and paper.

Unfortunately, this is not allowed. But I do not want you to be shocked or taken by surprise when you realise that anything you want out of your contract must be fought for, battled for, by you alone.

I find this totally unfair. Why should a young lad, fresh from two years of football apprenticeship, be subjected to an ordeal that brings him into direct confrontation, and possibly conflict, with experienced men, men who possess business knowledge that you do not possess? Son, look out for number one. Freedom of contract is just around the corner. I do not believe that footballers will get complete freedom of contract for a few years, but the semi-freedom that is about to become standard may do a lot to sweep away some of these disgraceful, cobwebbed clauses.

There is no doubt that to many people the word 'professional' still implies something seedy, grasping and even dirty. How often have you heard amateurs described as 'the true sportsmen' or 'the chaps who play the jolly old game, what,

what!' To be a professional in any field, especially sport, is to invite the sideways glances. The time has come for people to stop regarding professional sportsmen as athletic mercenaries. I, for one, am sick of the attitudes of adult people who really ought to know better.

When you sign your first contract, you will be deciding your weekly groceries, the size and price of your car, house and clothes bills. Yes, exactly the same daily and weekly responsibilities as the bank clerk salesman, train driver or fireman. So you should allow nobody to accuse you of being greedy or grasping because you demand a decent living wage and decent living standards.

The first point of your contract to consider is the amount of basic wages offered, then link that amount to the bonuses offered. Most clubs offer a win and draw bonus. But some clubs complicate their bonus system by including a crowd bonus – gauged by the size of the attendance at each match – and linking the crowd bonus to smaller win and draw bonuses.

There is certain to be a sum of money included in the contract known as appearance money. This is the amount automatically paid whenever you make an appearance in the first team, and brings your normal, reserve team basic nearer to the standard first-team basic, depending on how often you are called into the first team.

There are countless complications involved in a professional footballer's contract; and while the introduction of the freedom of contract proposals may help to improve it, I foresee even greater technical complications for the player to handle. This is why I advise you to bide your time and to consider every word written on your contract before signing. Go home and think about what you have read. Don't rush into signing anything until you have considered all the pros and cons.

A lot of the pressures that you will experience when you come to sign your contract stem directly from the pressures that burden the manager. He has been given a budget – a certain amount of money with which he must pay all the players' wages for the year. The board of directors tell the manager that the money he has is all he is going to get. So the manager has to pay out this money in whatever proportions per individual he deems to be correct.

This is just one factor you will have to overcome if you are not satisfied with what you are offered. What you may not realise is that the manager may have used up his money by offering you a contract in the first place. So now the battle is on. You must fight for what you believe you are worth. The manager, who would probably pay his players the earth if he had the money, has to put on the cold, hard businessman's face, and fight to get you on contract for the lowest annual wage he can get away with. This is where the pecking order plays such a major part. The manager must always answer to the board of directors in the end. He is more than likely not in a position to give you what you want or even what he himself believes you to be worth. Because the source of the money demanded is upstairs ... and they say, 'No more dough.'

Weigh up everything. What are your prospects of getting into the first team? How much will you earn in a year in the reserve team without appearance money? What will your earnings be after one year in the reserves? Do not settle for today. Think of tomorrow.

There is another good reason for biding your time. How many young players have jumped at signing a professional contract with the first club who approached them? Too many. And why? Because nobody bothers to knock out of them the servile attitude that leaves them grateful for the opportunity and grateful to the club for even asking.

Think of yourself as the best. You are going to be a winner. You are going to make clubs grateful to you for signing with them!

Too many lads have signed on the dotted line without waiting for those important two or three days – the time it might take another club to step in and offer them a better contract and a more secure future. I am not saying that the contract offered to you is automatically a poor one. But I am

41

saying, take nothing for granted. It is quite possible that the first club to ask you to join them will make you the best offer of all time, and that the clubs who come in later will not be prepared to match that first offer. If that is your good fortune, then grasp the opportunity. But check before you leap.

The next question is – how long a contract should you sign? It appears that options are the first things to be scrapped once freedom of contract comes in. At least players will have the choice of including the option in their contract. Mind you, any player who deliberately asks for the option clause to be included in his contract deserves no sympathy.

So, with the option out of the way, you have the choice. You must base that choice on the fact that you have ability, and the confidence in your ability to do well in your first year. So why should you sign a contract for more than one year?

If you, when offered your first contract, do not have confidence in your own ability then I suggest you forget about signing anything and get out of the game.

Make sure that you hold whatever options are going – and hold those options over the club. Do not tie yourself down for more than one year at a time. Stay on as short a contract as possible while you are young. The time to begin looking for a long contract is when your career has reached its peak and is beginning to wane.

This brings us on to another very important aspect of the economic side of professionalism: pension schemes. When a lad of eighteen or nineteen is signing his first contract and his professional career appears to spread in front of him, he is unlikely to think of things such as pension schemes. But I believe that this is the very time to see to such things. I know it always seems that there are years ahead, years to be experienced and enjoyed, before thinking in terms of a pension. But the years fly by, especially in so demanding a profession, and you can be in football and on your way out of the game before you realise that your career is really over.

The day when you know that your professional career is slowly ending is the day when you begin to wonder if you have made enough money out of your playing career to secure your non-playing future. Never forget that your career could end – as did that of Charlton Athletic goalkeeper Graham Tutt – before it even gets off the ground. Tutt, at twenty, was injured in a match at Sunderland. He put up a brave fight, but medical opinion outweighed all his efforts, and the facial injury he received while diving at the feet of striker Tom Finney ended his career.

This could happen to you. In any match, in a five-a-side or in a training match kickabout session. Nothing is assured in football except the fact that you will get old and that your career will end. Hopefully, it ends somewhere around your early thirties; but even then, you have, hopefully, as long again and a bit more to live. Are you sure that you have sufficient resources to live comfortably, to keep your wife and children in the same secure position they held while you were hitting the headlines as a player?

Pensions are also, of course, very good ways of offsetting the heavy tax burden that young players face. You can build a tidy little sum over the ten to thirteen years of your career if your career spans that period – and be in a position to start your own small business when your playing career ends.

Unfortunately, too many footballers think it their God-given right to earn money. So it comes as a nasty blow when, at the age of thirty-two, they are not wanted by their club. The blow becomes a numbing shock when they then discover that they cannot find a position with another club. All of a sudden they realise that the good life they had, and the money that was always in their pocket, are no longer there. Now they have to face up to that awful reality – they have to go out and work for their living.

Hangers-on are no help. In fact they are a pest, a scourge and a danger to you throughout your career. I'm talking of ever-present back-slappers who remind young players of their status constantly, exhaustingly, until these lads begin to live with their heads in the clouds. To them, tomorrow will never come. How often have I heard hangers-on say to a player: 'Don't you worry, son, I'll look after you when you finish playing.' What you must always remember is that these people only want to know you when you are doing well – when you are a personality, a name, a means by which they may bask in reflected glory. The day you go a bit down on your uppers, these people disappear with the speed of a community fleeing from a plague epidemic.

Never rely on anybody, in or out of football. Look after yourself. Make what you can out of your profession – and be totally fair to it in return. Put into your profession as much as you take out. Put in more if you possibly can. Be honest, be straight. Do not suffer fools gladly. Follow these simple guidelines and you will become a well-respected figure within the game.

While we are discussing football as a business, I would like to give you some serious advice concerning any business ventures that catch your eye during your career.

Many players, at some stage or another, consider becoming involved in a business outside football. Usually they see such a move as a step in the right direction towards securing their living when they finish playing. This is all very well, providing they know what they are going into and with whom they are working. If all the ingredients are right, then no player can do a wiser thing than go into business and make a niche for himself later on in life.

But you must be aware of the pitfalls in this situation as well. I strongly advise you not to become involved in any venture into which you are invited. If someone with whom you are not well acquainted asks you to become a partner in a garage, shop, market stall or any form of business, I advise you to politely, but firmly, refuse.

Even if you know the person very well, do you know them well enough to put your hard-earned money into their hands while you are still totally concerned with football? To trust a person under such circumstances, that person would need to be a genuine, close friend. Even then, for the sake of mutual peace of mind, you and your friend should see to your own legal arrangements so that there can be no 'misunderstandings' – ever.

This is not hardness or meanness. Nobody respects a fool. But there are plenty of people around only too willing to fleece a fool. Don't be a fool. Lay it on the line from the beginning. Set the standards, and hammer anyone who breaks those standards. A few people will think twice about crossing you, a few more will possibly even give you a wide berth. But nobody will dare show you any disrespect in business dealings.

If going into business is of your own choosing, but you haven't the time to set everything up, you must choose the person with whom you are prepared to share your business. This is the most difficult part of the whole operation. Not setting up the business, but finding the right person to partner. So many footballers, some of them leading names in England, have gone into business and been fiddled, conned and downright robbed. They have lost virtually everything and spent the rest of their careers paying off debts – simply because of their choice of business partner.

There are plenty of courses open to footballers who want to establish a career outside the game. Unfortunately, not enough footballers attend these courses. Yet they, more than any other members of society, have the time on their hands to go to college or even attempt home correspondence courses.

Business management is an excellent subject to study. Take my advice. If you have any plans about going into business either during or after your playing career, make the effort and go to college. You will reap the benefits tenfold when the time comes to face the responsibilities and problems of the business world. And if you are fortunate enough to stay in the game as a coach or manager when you finish playing, you will still realise the benefits of having completed a course in business management. Because you will be deeply involved in man management. Whether you open your own business outside football or whether you stay in the game, you will have to deal with people at a variety of levels.

Don't join the moronic majority who spend their spare

time in snooker halls, at racetracks or sitting with square eyes watching the women's programmes on television during the early afternoon. Put your time to positive use. Exercise your brain. You will find that during your football-working day you will have plenty of opportunities to exercise your body, but never forget the brain.

Now we can move on to tackle the playing side of professionalism.

I make no apologies for returning to a point, made earlier in this chapter, concerning the attitude of so many people to the word 'professional'. Because you must come to terms with this attitude the moment you sign on the dotted line and join the professional football ranks. Sadly, the word 'professional' is viewed by a large section of the public as something akin to a swear word, something almost dirty. Equally sad is the fact that many of those people have reason to dislike the very sound of the word. I have said that this attitude annoys and frustrates me, but I am also bound to admit that certain aspects of 'professionalism', or what people outside looking in deem to be professionalism, are not to be admired, least of all by you, the reader.

You must understand the difference between being professional and being mercenary. The true meaning of the word 'professional', from the point of view of the sportsman, is not just the division that separates the unpaid sportsman and the paid sportsman: the money aspect is only part of the spectrum.

Entering the world of the professional footballer, you must be prepared to alter considerably a lot of your mental attitudes and physical capabilities. You must work towards perfecting a mind and body capable of withstanding the traumas and pressures of the professional world. These pressures do exist; they are not just the backdoor excuse for tired sportsmen, as so many people outside the game believe. Once you have achieved this higher level of mental and physical endurance, you must maintain it, extracting the utmost from your own resources for your profession – which is the ideal way of keeping mental and physical levels high and in tune.

As I have said, it is not just a matter of money. There are many 'professional amateurs' leading their fields in world sport. Take, for example, Lasse Viren, the world-famous Finnish long-distance runner. Viren has created, within his mind and body, what is known as 'the killer instinct'. His approach to a race is totally professional in so far as he has done all his homework, knows the strength of the field, knows the twists, turns and wind-breaks of the course. And he has made his mind up that he is going to win. When his body aches for rest, Viren's mind keeps cool and maintains control until the objective has been achieved: victory. Dedicated, determined, he is a man with the will to win, the obsession that he must be the best – a professional in skill and experience who has no thoughts whatsoever of money when he pounds around the last lung-bursting lap towards the tape of which he has dreamed for weeks.

Alan Ball summed up what I am explaining to you when he said: 'When I go out on the pitch, I have no friends. I have respect for fellow professionals, certainly. But no friends. I'm out there to do a job, and I'll always do well, in any team, at any level. Why? Because when I'm playing, I am a nasty, horrible little so-and-so. I upset people, I chat them, niggle them. I want to play. Most of all I want to win. I'm not talking about foul play, nasty tackles or obscene language – but about getting one up on the opposition, always being a step ahead, always being first with the pass, the interception, the tackle, the shot. Always going out to be the winner.' These are the words of the true professional.

After the match, Alan Ball is one of the most genial men I have ever met. He enjoys a good old chat with his team-mates and with members of the opposition – perhaps sharing a lager with the very player he has spent most of the afternoon battling to outdo!

There is no malice. There must be no malice. We are all in the one profession. When everyone in our profession wants to be a winner, that is when our profession will become different

47

class. Unfortunately, too many modern professionals are either not bothered or are happy with their lot and lack ambition.

When you go out on that pitch, keep one thing uppermost in your mind – you have got to win the game. Nothing else is as important as that one objective. You are not out there to have a good time, nor to show the Dunkirk spirit and celebrate defeat like a 'jolly good chap ought to'.

Grit your teeth, hate every moment that you don't have the ball. Hate every opponent – for as long as the match lasts. Be a hundred-per-cent winner who is not interested in being a satisfied loser – an 'almost made it, but not quite' character. We have too many of them as it is.

So much for the overall attitude. But the attitude I have just described is nothing more than a theatrical sham unless the whole mental and physical attitude is totally professional from the beginning. Playing at being a winner is easy to do – make a few faces, wave your arms around like a windmill when you dive in for balls you cannot possibly reach. I think I have painted enough of that picture for you to complete the canvas.

No, being a winner is as much an attitude of mind as it is a combination of attitudes to situations out on the pitch. To win a game, you must win countless situations throughout the ninety minutes. Only if you win these situations will the final result be in your favour. Every time a tackle is lost your team are pushed a little closer to the brink of defeat. Every time a bad pass is delivered, a poor cross dispatched or a header misdirected – all these situations combined can lead to ultimate defeat.

So you see that winning is more than just being a member of the team who snatched victory, against the run of play. Winning is something you aim for every day of the week, every day you get up.

I once played in a testimonial match at Sunderland for their winger, Billy Hughes. The match itself was a cracker. But it was something said to me before the match that provides the perfect example I require. Testimonial games are

48

looked upon by most people as occasions for a bit of light-hearted relief – games in which the players relax, stroke the ball about, have some fun and earn a few laughs from the crowd. But the true professional will have none of this. On the occasion in question Bobby Charlton was playing in the same side as myself, and he quickly set the scene by saying a few well-chosen words just before we went out on the pitch.

'Now look, lads, people have paid hard-earned money to see a good match. So let's give them something to talk about.' Almost immediately, all chat ceased and the rest of the players became quiet and serious. He added: 'By the way, I have never played in a losing team at Sunderland and I don't want to start tonight. OK?'

Bobby Charlton was as good as his word. We stormed around for ninety minutes, played very well, and thumped Sunderland 6-3! That is what being a professional is all about. The pride in your position and in your profession should be all the motivation you require to play to the best of your ability.

I often make my judgements of players, particularly those with whom I am playing, during training sessions. I believe that training should be looked upon with the same professional attitude and killer-instinct as afforded to actual games. I want you to remember this throughout your professional career. You cannot switch your winning lust on and off like a tap.

Training sessions maintain levels of fitness and sharpness. They also generate team-spirit within a squad. But players must use them to the full if they want to maintain their professional standards and hone their professional instincts. The training session is the time for getting into the habit of doing the correct thing. It is foolhardy to expect to get away with only going through the motions during training, and then be able to find top gear on match day.

For example, nothing infuriates me more than the lack of killer instinct shown by so many footballers during practice matches and training exercises, such as forwards against

49

defence. The opening moves are always satisfactory, even promising. A player knocks the ball on to a colleague and goes past one or two defenders to receive the return pass. Now he has got in behind the defence and has only the goalkeeper to beat. More often than not, the player rounds off his good approach work by tapping the ball casually to the goalkeeper.

To me, the whole exercise is a waste of time unless that ball is stuck in the back of the net, because on match-day, the one-two will come off a treat but when the forward comes to beating the goalkeeper, he suddenly discovers that this is something he does very rarely – and probably misses a good scoring chance. This whole attitude is downright bad professionalism. This is the example of a player satisfied to have beaten the defender and when he is through, with only the goalkeeper to beat, the job, to him, has already been done – so he tamely rolls the ball away and returns to his original position.

This is like the gunfighter who proudly struts around the town, wearing his new outfit – all leather with silver buttons – and his new guns – pearl-handled Colt 45s with solid silver bullets. He looks the part, he acts the part. He is most of the way towards being the part. That is, until some scruffy cowboy, who spends day after day shooting bottles off a wall, draws and shoots to kill while the gunslinger is admiring his appearance in a shop window.

What price has that player got when he comes face to face with an opposing goalkeeper? He is still able to play a sweet one-two, but he lacks sharpness in front of goal, because he has abused training sessions – sessions when he should have taken shots at goal at every opportunity.

Getting into scoring positions is only half the job. Scoring is the other half – the most important half. Unfortunately, too many players believe that it is nasty to keep sticking the ball past their own goalkeeper in training session. Rubbish! He needs the practice and so do they. The goalkeeper is not going to face forwards who roll the ball to him when they have completed the fancy part of their approach work and the strikers will only become 'killers' when they learn to stick the ball in the net as if by reflex action rather than premeditation.

Yes, be nasty in training. Beat your team-mates in tackles, challenges and sprints. Belt the ball past your own goal-keeper every chance you get. Make your team-mates look bad players if you can. Get them riled to the extent where they are out to make you look a bad player. Now we've got some winning instincts roused!

The training sessions are the perfect opportunities for you to show up the weaknesses of your team-mates. You must hope that they show up your weaknesses also. Far better to spotlight your various weak spots during club training than to have them exposed by the opposition on match-day. If a team-mate does show up your weaknesses, don't get sore. Don't ruck and argue. Just paw the ground until dust swirls up around you, flare your nostrils and take them all to the cleaners. Show them their own blind-spots, weak spots, slow spots and their Achilles heels.

The real professional is constantly striving to become better. He is never fully satisfied with his lot in life. He is never ready to say: 'I've made it this time. I can't go any further.' Perhaps he can't go any further up the ladder in his career. But that does not mean that he ceases to strive. The true professional works and grafts all the time to improve his skills and his knowledge of football. He is always ready to discuss the game, listen to points of view, thrash out points of interest, slam down wafflers who attempt to jump on the bandwagon with a little semi-professional education. No pro can tolerate outsiders who attempt to tell him about football.

It is often the outsider who takes a look and singles out the wrong player as the 'model professional'. The test is when the outsider's choice and the choice of another professional are compared.

Often I have heard people describe players as 'the type of player my son should watch and whose example my son should follow.' Maybe, but then it depends on what you want your son to be. Have you recognised the type of player

51

to which I am referring? Wonderful club servant. Does not drink. Never smokes. Clean living (whatever that means depends on whether the 'judge' is thinking in terms of morals or soap). Joined us from school and has played for us for fifteen years, doing a good, solid and reliable job.

But I immediately stick a big question mark after the name of that player. Because I ask myself: 'Is he really a good professional?' The alternative is that he is one of those people who reach a certain level in football, achieve a certain status and are content to cling to their security instead of pushing on up the ladder at every given opportunity.

Harsh? Cynical? Not really. There are people who shy away from going higher because they are afraid of being found out. So is the so-called 'model professional' really a man who is afraid of moving on, afraid of stepping out of line to further his own career, a man afraid of leaving the world he has built around himself? If so, then he is no professional at all.

Having said this, I do not want you to adopt a cynical attitude towards every one-club player you meet. Geoff Hurst is a good example of the model pro who is exactly that – a model for all young players. Common sense will tell you that I am not sweeping a net across all the one-club men in football. Many are brilliant professionals. But there are those who hide behind the guise of a model career, and while they cause no ripples, let alone waves, they also contribute little in the way of stimulating their own profession.

Find your club by all means. Stick by that club if you are happy and well treated. But never allow your happiness to develop into a lazy contentment. Fight and graft to be better every day. Improve your technique, practise on your own if you believe it will help you to sharpen one aspect of your play. Set your standards, then not only maintain them but aim to improve them throughout your career.

Now I come to that aspect of 'professionalism' that no true professional will tolerate. It has to do with cheating. It has to do with cowardice. And it often leads to the whole professional game being tarred with a dirty brush. I am talking about the so-called 'professional tackle', or, as it is known in the game, 'going over the top'.

This is where, in a fifty-fifty or sixty-forty situation in which two players are going towards each other with the ball in the middle, one player raises his boot above the level of the ball and brings his boot down on the knee, shin or foot of his opponent. The momentum of his foot is then stopped, and often he can drag his foot back, bringing the ball with him. There are some absolute 'masters' of this dirty little trick who make it appear they have won a perfectly fair tackle – and who have left many a cripple lying on the ground.

Never, never describe the 'over-the-top tackle' as the professional tackle. The true professional tackle is where one player goes in, hard and fair, and wins the ball in a straightforward challenge for possession with an opponent.

If a player makes an over-the-top tackle on you, do not retaliate in kind. Get up – if you can – and show that cheat just how good a player you are and how futile are his attempts to kick you out of your stride. You will win, he will lose – and you will be seen to be the true professional.

FOUR

A Time for Work

The Greats, and how to use them

Your education must change gear dramatically between the ages of seventeen and twenty. It is very important that you watch good players in action. Equally important, you must be accompanied by your coach, manager or a senior player when you go to watch a match. In these years you must be taught how to *use* great players – how to appreciate their skills, their techniques and their weaknesses. Yes, every footballer has weaknesses in his game, even the greatest.

What matters to you is that you understand everything you see. That is why I stress the importance of being accompanied by a properly qualified football coach, manager or player. I know that many youngsters enjoy going to football matches with their fathers. There is nothing wrong with this. Of course not. Fathers, with the best will in the world, want their sons to believe that dad is every bit as knowledgeable as any club coach. But that very desire on the part of the enthusiastic father can lead to a bad education on the part of the young boy.

I watched Fulham playing in a home game when I was a schoolboy, and something the legendary Johnny Haynes did left me bewildered. When I got home I asked my dad why so-and-so had done such-and-such, and why Haynes had played a certain pass instead of the pass I thought was on. I expected an immediate reply and solution. Boys always do when they throw such a teaser at their dad. But my father said: 'Get a pencil, draw the pitch, and pinpoint the twenty-two players and where they were when so-and-so did such-

and-such.' I began to explain when he interrupted me: 'Don't tell me what happened around the ball, son, tell me what happened around the rest of the pitch.' My father was making it painfully clear that I had not watched the game or fully understood what was happening. I had followed the progress of the ball and remembered only what happened in the immediate vicinity of the ball, forgetting to watch the whole pitch and all the players.

How many football supporters do exactly the same thing, especially when the ball reaches the penalty area and the excitement builds up? You, if left to your own devices, would do exactly as I did.

How many fathers would have puffed out their chests and said: 'Well, son, it's simple really. When you've seen as many games as I have, incidents such as this are easier to understand ... blah, blah, blah.'

The situation is commonplace. The boy looks up to his dad, his dad grows a few feet in stature for an evening, and the next day, he says to his pals: 'I know I'm right ... my dad says ...'

That incident with my father highlights the kind of situation you will face, and how mistaken you will be if you watch matches as part of your education, without the assistance of a qualified person.

When I played for Luton Town, the club coach, then Jimmy Andrews, accompanied me to countless matches. Every time I went to a match, I concentrated all my attention on one player. I noted where my 'player of the day' ran, and his reactions to those around him, and I asked why. I watched his running off the ball, and asked how. I made mental notes of all the aspects of his play that I understood, and made written notes of all the points I did not understand. At the end of the match I bombarded Jimmy Andrews with questions. I also challenged his answers. I was not suggesting that Jimmy was incorrect on any point. But if a shadow of a doubt remained in my mind, then I let Jimmy know.

I remember going to watch West Ham United play in a

55

home match. I can't recall the opposition, but then I was only at Upton Park for one reason: to watch Geoff Hurst.

Hurst was not a natural forward. By that I mean no disrespect to a great player. Hurst was one of the greats. He achieved his greatness as a front-runner through hard work, by listening and learning and by watching other players in action. And he always asked questions!

Hurst began his career as a wing-half. But Ron Greenwood spotted his potential as a striker and Hurst proved an ideal and willing pupil.

During the match I watched, a West Ham defender intercepted a pass and began racing up the wing. Hurst, close-marked by a defender, made a run into space, checked back, then checked out again. He lost his marker for long enough to provide the player on the ball with a clear target. The attacking player, however, retained possession and kept his head down. He was unaware of Hurst's efforts.

Hurst made another run, this time in the opposite direction, checking back, checking out again. He must have covered over 100 yards in short, sharp, exhausting sprints in a matter of seconds. Three times he provided his team-mate with a good target. Three times he had to shrug his shoulders and shake his head in despair. By this time the attacking player had looked up, completely misread Hurst's intentions and passed the ball all the way back to Bobby Moore.

I doubt if more than five people in what was a five-figure crowd either saw or understand the extent to which Hurst had worked to create space and to accept the responsibility of possession from a team-mate while under pressure.

Throughout his distinguished career, Geoff Hurst remained a model professional. How sad that so much of his incredible work went unnoticed and unheralded.

My point is that I would have missed a lot of Hurst's work that night had Jimmy Andrews not been by my shoulder. After I had fired my questions, Jimmy questioned me on what I had seen, then made the necessary corrections. Later, I watched Johnny Haynes, Denis Law, Jimmy Greaves and Roger Hunt. I watched other great players in action. But I always had professional assistance, otherwise I would have wasted my time, incapable alone of telling the real thing from a phoney.

You have now reached a major crossroads in your career. You can carry on as you are, training, playing and working hard – or you can broaden your horizons as well. You can accept that you are so close to and yet so far from knowing what football is all about.

You have a lot to learn. You have to buckle down to learning. I do not wish to give the impression that you can only learn from great players. You have a mind of your own: you must use it. Without such individual minds producing new and individual thoughts, football would never go forwards.

Nor am I advocating that you should go out of your way to become a football rebel. But you must ask questions. You must make decisions. You must think for yourself as well as accept advice and help from others. You must analyse the good, bad and farcical aspects of everything you learn about football. The master is not *always* correct, nor is the pupil *always* wrong. *Ask those questions.*

The secret of benefiting from a good education is to be attentive, accept criticism, assessing all the reasons behind it, and be prepared to throw back points that do not immediately make sense.

I strongly advise you to make an effort to join your school debating class at some stage of your school career. I believe that the more opportunities you receive to practise the art of debate and discussion, the better will be your chances of getting to grips with football question-and-answer sessions. And in later life, you will be faced with such discussions in the changing-room, at home, in the pub, clubhouse and the local supermarket. Be prepared. The day you begin your professional career, you will be surrounded, endlessly, by experts – some genuine, some close to the truth and a hell of a lot of cardboard cut-outs whose football knowledge is based on cigarette cards and comics.

Some people will be genuine, friendly and eager to help.

Others will knock you down with criticism, mostly incredibly off-beam rubbish. Never be too affected by either camp. Be your own man, believe in your ability, your brain and your integrity.

There are twenty basic qualities applicable to the professional footballer. I list them in the table below.

1	Instant ball control.
2	Heading ability (attacking headwork and defensive headwork).
3	Control of the ball at speed.
4	Vision and passing.
5	Space creation.
6	Balance under pressure.
7	Shooting.
8	Dribbling.
9	Crossing.
10	Goal poaching.
11	Tackling.
12	The ability to organise other players.
13	Shielding the ball.
14	Running off the ball.
15	Tactical appreciation.
16	Positional sense.
17	Curling the ball (the moving ball and the dead ball).
18	Bravery.
19	Fitness.
20	Handling crosses and good reflexes.

You must know which of these qualities are your strongest and which are your weakest. But you must not work on your weak points at the direct expense of your strengths. Too many so-called experts emphasise the need to be an all-round player. In other words they are trying to produce a pack of 'Jack-of-all-trades' who are truly masters of none. If your right foot is good and your heading work is good, why should you spend valuable time trying to make your left foot as good as your right? Better, surely, to work on your strengths until that right foot is one of the best in football; until your heading is second to none. Work on weak points by all means. Never go to extremes. But do not fall into the age-old trap of believing that you must have excellence beaming out of all ten toes.

If I have two houses to sell, one saleable and one which is proving difficult to sell, which house do I sell first? Naturally, I sell the house that can be sold, and then begin to worry about the other house. A simple analogy maybe. But my message is clear enough.

A well-known Fleet Street journalist once criticised my game and advised me to: 'Learn how to kick with your right foot.' When I replied that I would gladly oblige the moment he wrote his next match-report with his left hand, he accepted my touché, albeit grudgingly.

Returning to my list of twenty qualities – there are a few headings that require a lot of extra thought. Bravery, for example, is a quality that is best left to others to judge. In any case, an honest player will know whether or not he is brave. He does not need to write it down among his qualities.

Honesty is, in itself, a form of bravery. No player enjoys admitting a weakness – least of all to himself. But now comes question time!

Having studied the list of twenty qualities, and having accepted that each and every quality could fill a chapter on its own, you must be completely honest and brutal with yourself when you select your strong points. Otherwise the whole exercise is a waste of time. There must be none of this 'I'm not bad at heading' or 'My passing is getting better'. You must sit down and draw up your list. You must select your *real* strengths, ignoring the temptation to add those 'not quite sure on that one' qualities.

I expect you to come up with three or four good points. Now you are in business. A major step has been taken: you know in which direction you are going.

There is no such thing as a perfect footballer. Such a man

would need to comprise all twenty of the ideal pro's qualities, and that would give the word 'bionic' a new dimension. Therefore it is reasonable to accept that any footballer who possesses, in strength, three or four of the twenty, has what it takes to make the grade.

Let us assume that you select heading (defensively), balance, tackling and positional sense. All four qualities point to your being a natural centre-half. (When I first read such a list, I wrote down shooting, goal-poaching, controlling the ball at speed, and running off the ball. I was a centre-forward in the making.)

I appreciate that some of the twenty headings do overlap. For example, shooting and curling the ball could be viewed as separate strengths or a combined strength. Balance under pressure and shielding the ball can be united or separated, depending on where a player is, what situation he is in and how many players are around him.

Now that you have selected your strengths, you must watch the top players who possess and excel in those strengths.

For defensive heading watch Southampton centre-half Chris Nicholl, Manchester City's Dave Watson or Leeds' Gordon McQueen – three powerful, positive and direct central defenders who dominate in the air. For balance, there are few players to better Leeds' Tony Currie or my Arsenal team-mates 'Chippy' Brady and Alan Hudson. They all combine the art of shielding the ball when running and retaining their balance under pressure when cornered.

Chippy – so named because of his remarkable left foot – has perfected a knack which, at first, I believed to be nothing more than a matter of luck. He rides tackles in such a way that opponents knock the ball back on to Chippy's shins and he then directs the ball behind his opponent – and follows it. The ball rarely goes to the right or left of him when he is challenged for possession. It always appears to bounce straight into his path.

Alan Hudson has the brilliant knack of putting opponents on their backsides by a simple but deadly shift of balance and

60

a drop of the shoulder. These are examples of perfect balance. Such natural, instinctive skills are a must for you to watch. If you are going to be a centre-half you must learn about balance.

Tackling is an art in itself. I advise you to watch Arsenal's 'Stan' Simpson and Manchester City's Mike Doyle. Although they are entirely different in style, their timing and their respective methods are superb.

Positional sense is something every player needs. Therefore I suggest that you will learn all there is to know about positional sense from the players I have just mentioned.

There is another serious threat to your development: fantasies. One of the magical yet damaging aspects of professional football is that players live out the fantasies of their supporters.

As a schoolboy, I remember lying awake for hours, worrying about Fulham's match the next day. I wanted Johnny Haynes to do well. I lived every minute of a game that was still eighteen hours away, making every pass, challenging for every ball. Yet Haynes was having a perfectly good night's sleep while, like me, thousands of other Fulham supporters tossed and turned worrying for him.

This is all part of the magic. But in the context of your football future, the magic can also be harmful. You, for example, may be a Manchester City supporter. Every Saturday you stand on the terraces at Maine Road, cheering City and reserving a special cheer for Dennis Tueart, your idol. You want City to win, and long for Tueart to score. If Tueart does score, your arms, like those of the thousands of fans around you, are thrust into the air in a victory salute. Without doubt, Tueart celebrates his goal with a similar gesture of delight. The electric spark that arcs between the players and their fans completes the fantasy. Tueart's goal was scored by thousands of City fans. That is the magic of football. During such moments, nothing separates the player from the supporters. They experience the same feelings of exaltation, relief, satisfaction and sheer joy.

Now we come to the problem. You dream of playing for

City. You want to be another Tueart. You want to be fast, skilful, deadly around the penalty area and accurate when crossing the ball. Unfortunately, you are 6 feet, 2 inches tall and 12½ stone! One glance at the list of twenty qualities will tell you that you are a centre-half. But at this stage, the stage when players are idols, you have one thought in your head – to be another Tueart. The painful realisation that you can never emulate Tueart hits you with crippling force – often more mentally crippling than anyone around you understands. Without help, advice and understanding, you concentrate on the qualities you do not possess. You fret about the fact that you can never be a striking winger. You lose confidence, and can even convince yourself that you cannot play at all.

That kind of negative attitude is rife in football. It has always been a dangerous and harmful state of mind that can afflict a youngster who is battling, alone, to come to terms with his football capabilities, often in defiance of his youthful dreams. If you are not educated, you will never understand how to assess your strengths or how to develop those strengths. There is nothing wrong with following every step of Tueart's career – from the terraces. You should go on collecting those action pictures and pin them on your bedroom wall. We have all done exactly the same thing. But when you get to seventeen, you must set aside your spectator interests and examine your own career – establish your own strengths as opposed to longing for strengths you do not possess. Reality must hit the young professional early – and hit him hard.

You of those 6 feet, 2 inches and 12½ stone are a good centre-half in the making. Now is the time for you to accept that fact and get down to work. You will never dribble as Tueart dribbles. You will never score goals the way Tueart scores them. But given time and hard work, you will one day face a player of Tueart's capabilities and shut him out of a game. No offence to Dennis Tueart. I could have selected any player in Britain for this example. Nor am I establishing that you are that tall, that heavy or indeed a centre-half.

Having reached the conclusion that you are (in this example still) a centre-half, you know your strengths and your weaknesses. Now is the time for you to begin watching great players. No, I have not put the cart before the horse. I began by establishing the importance of watching great players. Then I discussed the twenty qualities. But there is method in my madness. I have deliberately switched the order of priority in order to wrap the two points together so they are seen to be inseparable.

Of course you must establish your strengths before you watch great players in action. There is no point in your watching countless strikers if you are a centre-half. This can happen. You may be still playing out of position at seventeen. If you are one of the unlucky youngsters – and there are many of them around – you may never get the opportunity to study such a list. You may never know your best position.

Geoff Hurst – in this instance – is a classic example. I doubt if Hurst would have remained in the First Division, let alone scored a hat-trick in a World Cup Final, had he continued as a moderate, hard-working wing-half. As I established, Ron Greenwood saw the potential and he wasted no time spelling out the situation to Hurst. What happened is now soccer history. I advise every schoolboy to take a close look at the career of Geoff Hurst, because he is a player whose example I would like every boy to follow.

I accept that going to a match and concentrating only on one player is difficult. The excitement of any match is enough to turn a spectator's head. But if you do not do your homework, or should I say 'matchwork', your failure to study will be reflected in your limitations. Oh yes, you will always have limitations. Every footballer has strong points and weak points. That includes the greats. The danger signals will flash, however, when you begin to show limitations in your strong points, in your best qualities. If you do not watch, listen, learn and question everything you see, you will throw away the opportunity of adding a whole new dimension to your game.

Working on the basis that you, the reader, want to begin

your 'matchwork' this weekend, I have repeated the list of twenty qualities, now adding the names of players I believe you ought to watch.

Qualities	Players
1 Instant ball control	Allan Clarke; George Best
2 Heading ability: defensive	Chris Nicholl; Dave Watson; Gordon McQueen
attacking	Andy Gray; John Toshack
3 Control of the ball at speed	Trevor Francis; George Best
4 Vision and passing	Alan Hudson; Terry Hibbitt
5 Space creation: negative	Alan Hudson
positive	Phil Boyer
6 Balance under pressure	Tony Currie; Liam Brady; Alan Hudson
7 Shooting	Peter Lorimer; Frank Worthington
8 Dribbling	Liam Brady; George Best
9 Crossing	Dave Thomas; Clive Woods
10 Goal poaching and scoring	Ted MacDougall; Allan Clarke; Andy Gray; Malcolm Macdonald
11 Tackling	Mike Doyle; Peter Simpson
12 Ability to organise other players	Alan Ball
13 Shielding	Tony Currie; Liam Brady; Alan Hudson
14 Running off the ball	Mike Channon; Phil Boyer
15 Tactical appreciation	Alf Ramsey; Dave Sexton; Alan Ball; Ron Greenwood; Malcolm Allison; Bobby Moore
16 Positional sense	All the players and managers on this list
17 Curling the ball	Tony Currie; Alan Hudson
18 Bravery	Andy Gray; Jimmy Rimmer
19 Fitness	Everyone on this list
20 Handling and crossing	Pat Jennings; Phil Parkes; Ray Clemence

These are the men I advise you to either watch or listen to. I admit that Dave Sexton and Alf Ramsey are a little difficult when it comes to communicating with people outside their immediate surrounds – nevertheless, they possess the football brains that cannot and must not be ignored.

Now to clear up those questions you are longing to ask. What do I mean by space creation, positive and negative? In a nutshell, Alan Hudson has the ability to create space for himself in and around his own half and even in his own area. This is *negative* space creation.

Phil Boyer excels at *positive* space creation because he works so well in the opposition's half and around their area. The space Hudson creates provides him with room in which to play. He is therefore always available as an outlet for a pass. Boyer makes space for either himself or for other forwards. The result of his work is more likely to create a goal-chance. More about this subject later.

As you may have gathered by now, I believe passionately in this method of educating young players. From the ages of seventeen – and even sixteen in certain cases – to twenty, 'matchwork' is a must in a young footballer's programme of development. My adherence to this method stems, very simply, from the fantastic wealth of new knowledge I acquired by watching Law, Hurst, Greaves, Hunt and the others of my 'student' days. I see no point in writing a chapter containing self-indulgent waffle about these players, their greatest games, what they said after such-and-such a game, etc, etc. Such ramblings would serve no practical purpose, certainly not as far as your career is concerned. Too often have I listened to arguments developing in dressing-rooms between the present players and past players – endless circles of waffle about the great players of their particular heyday. It serves no practical purpose when simply thrown around the shower room as blatant nostalgic ramblings.

All the same, thirty years of mellowing will always make yesteryear 'the good old days'. When I think of a heading such as 'The Greats', I immediately picture a young professional whose eyes are glued to the movements and style of a great player. My gauge of a great player is very simple. How many young players have become better players by watching the great player? To me, that is the one true measure of greatness in this profession.

FIVE

The Physiology of Football

One of the greatest mental stresses a professional footballer can suffer stems from the physical strains and stresses his job entails. The most heartbreaking period of time he ever has to endure is when he gets a serious injury, and knows that he is going to be out of the game for a long time.

When I say 'serious injury' I mean a broken limb, ligament or cartilage trouble or any of the countless pulls and strains that can halt, and sometimes wreck, a professional footballer's career. Once having sustained the injury, he must keep himself as fit as possible – without exerting undue pressure or stress on the injured area. When the injury begins to heal, the player wants to begin the long, hard and lonely slog of getting back to match-fitness. This is when he experiences a period in his life similar to that portrayed in the film *The Loneliness of the Long Distance Runner*. Most of his work will be done in an atmosphere of timeless solitude. If he does occasionally have company, it will probably be the club physiotherapist urging him on, pushing him towards the fitness he seeks.

During this battle to regain his fitness, the player has to work harder than at any other time in his football career. His fight is made that much more difficult because there is very little light at the end of his immediate tunnel. This applies most of all if his injury does not respond to treatment as quickly as he expects. This is something you must understand before you set your sights on a career in professional football. This is one of the less publicised, less dramatised sides of the profession. The day you receive such an injury, wait and wait for the go-ahead to resume light training, begin your battle in the gym or up and down the empty terraces, is the day your professional mettle will be tested to the full. And your loneliness will not be made any easier when you see the fit lads going out, doing their normal training – training most footballers enjoy, finishing with a five-a-side game.

Your mind is occupied with one thought and one thought only – the ball. The ball is what your whole life is about. This is the agonising period in your life when you never see a ball, and if you see one, you cannot touch it. You must complete the most testing fitness routines every day, seven days a week. There are no days off when you are injured. During this time, you see your team-mates pushing the ball around, doing all the things which come so naturally – that is, until the body cries out for repair.

Very little sympathy will come from your team-mates. Although it is true to say that going through their minds is 'But for the grace of God, there go I,' they know that tomorrow it could be their lot. It is a professional hazard, an intrinsic part of the footballer's way of life.

A great danger to the young professional is not knowing the extent of minor injuries. It is the minor injuries that can lead to a lot of problems later in his career.

When the young footballer begins to get the occasional pulls and strains in the early period of his career, he must know enough about his own body to gauge the amount of rest necessary to allow the injury to heal. If he doesn't know this, he may attempt to shrug it off as something that will pass with little bother. Of course he will receive expert medical care and help, but he is the only person who can feel the extent of his injury – and the extent of the healing process. Trouble arises when he is unable to interpret what he is feeling.

The danger lies in your enthusiasm for Saturday's match. What you consider to be a simple pull or strain may require days of rest to heal properly. But because you are young and probably do not know any better, you will play at all costs. In the long term, the cost can be very high.

The situation with most young footballers is that they have never encountered the pain-barrier. They are scared to cry 'chicken' or 'wolf' by saying: 'No, I don't think I'm fit enough to play,' or: 'No, I'm not fit enough to train.'

Too many coaches enter treatment rooms, take a quick glance at the injured man on the treatment table, turn to the physiotherapist and say: 'All he needs is a couple of hours' stiff training.' The coach, being senior to the physiotherapist – which is the case in many clubs – dominates the situation. The lad has to climb down off the treatment table, go out on the training field and work. Too many coaches believe that two hours' work-out does a muscle strain the world of good.

This is not a harsh or cruel judgement. It is because coaches are not medical men. Ask any member of the medical staff at any League club and he will tell you that the biggest curse is not a broken leg or a cartilage operation – the biggest curse, from his point of view, is the football coach.

Usually, the young player will experience a sense of fear – probably fear through respect for the coach. Therefore, he does as he is told without question, not wanting to say: 'But it really hurts.' In a physical game such as football, one is very careful not to cry 'chicken', or at least not cry it too often. You will experience this conflict at some stage in your career. You will be in pain. You will do as you are told. You will come to the brink of telling the coach that you are in pain, but the chances are that you will say nothing, or say that your injury is less serious than it really is, therefore misleading everyone. You will not want to give the impression that you are unable to keep up with the professional standards. Sadly, the standards, in this situation, leave a lot to be desired. But until you know this to be the case, your early years in the game will be punctuated by such conflicts.

Young footballers, just like the majority of people in every walk of life, do not understand the workings of the human body. But then neither do a lot of senior professional footballers, or indeed, a lot of coaches. Yet such knowledge is essential to the well-being of players.

68

You have probably never experienced real pain. Therefore you have no levels by which to gauge the seriousness of any knock or pull. If something hurts, you have no way of knowing whether it hurts a little, that much more or it's bloody agony. So what do you say to your coach on a Thursday morning when he asks: 'Coming out for training? You'd better come if you want to play on Saturday.' You will think of the pain, think of Saturday's match, and you will probably train. Having a fit young body, you will probably not over-aggravate the injury through training or through playing. You will gradually overcome the injury – but only in the short-term. The long-term is: will the injured area stay weak because it was never allowed to heal properly? Will arthritis set in during your post-career life? Yes, it is as serious as that. Your whole life can be ruined.

Too many players ignore the knocks and bruises they get. They do not report these 'little' injuries. But as far as I am concerned, it is far better for injuries to be rested on the Monday and Tuesday of the following week. The players who have suffered them should spend those two days receiving the correct treatment on the physio's table instead of training as if nothing were wrong. Two days of rest make all the difference. They ensure that instead of being ninety-per-cent fit, the player is one-hundred-per-cent fit. He can play on Saturday with the confidence of knowing that his injury has healed.

If you are ninety or even ninety-five per cent, you may believe you are fine – until you feel the slightest little twinge during the pre-match warm-up. Now your mind is unable to keep off that injured area. You are aware of it for the rest of the match. You will not push that injured part of your body. You will appear to go into tackles as you normally do, but when it comes to the crunch, you'll just pull out that little bit. That is the tiny percentage by which your team-mates have been let down, and it could mean the difference between winning and losing to a late goal. If an important member of the team has an injury that requires a couple of matches' rest, surely it is better to be without him in those two than in four or six matches later, when his half-healed injury deteriorates.

There are coaching courses which young players can attend which not only deal with the tactics of the game, but teach the students something about the human body. I believe it is about time managers and coaches made more of these courses. They are invaluable to young players, especially those aged between seventeen and twenty-three. Too many youngsters either hear about these courses third-hand without receiving the proper encouragement to attend, or never hear about them at all. This has got to stop! Young players deserve a better education.

You must understand how your body functions under stress, and what your body needs in the way of fuel – nutritional value – to allow you to succeed under stress. You need to know how much protein your body requires and, equally, how much carbohydrate. The human body is the most complicated piece of machinery ever seen on this earth – the most perfect engine, the most complex computer. To succeed in the professional game, you must know exactly how to keep this machinery ticking over in perfect tune, with all the parts properly oiled, fuelled and maintained.

Your future in football depends entirely on the condition of your body. If you are unable to keep your body in peak condition, it will let you down, sooner or later. And in your battle to overcome this let-down, you are in danger of damaging your body to such an extent that you will be forced to stop playing sooner than you expected – and may end your life a cripple.

I want you to understand the importance of fitness, and what the word actually means. Forcing your body to complete a training routine, going against nature by fighting pain, is no sign of fitness – or of masculinity. Perhaps sheer stupidity might be one description; crass ignorance another.

The slightest knock, the most 'trivial' pull, must be reported to the physiotherapist immediately. Swift action can mean the difference between two days of light treatment and rest, and two weeks' graft to repair a torn muscle, made worse because it was forced to work before it had healed.

A footballer can receive an injury in any one of a hundred ways. But accepting that, there are also certain 'danger areas' which must be guarded against.

There is nothing you can do if an opponent kicks you or causes you to fall awkwardly, twisting a knee or an ankle. But you can and must guard against pulling muscles or straining tendons because your body is thrust into action 'cold'. Before a game, or before a training session, it is vitally important that the body is warmed up. All vital parts of the body must be stretched so that when under stress, no muscles will be pulled.

Especially important to the footballer is the hamstring and the groin. Without the correct warming-up exercises, these two parts of his body could cause him a great deal of trouble. Both are used when stretching for the ball, kicking, running and sprinting. These are the occasions when serious damage can be caused, but all other parts of the body can suffer damage, quite possibly damage that you would not know about until later in your career.

I want to take you through a proper warm-up routine. I say proper because I imagine you doing a few press-ups, two or three high kicks, running on the spot and attempting to bring your knees to your chest. There are hundreds of these so-called exercises. What you require is a specific routine designed to benefit all the important parts of your body. The exercises I have described are, in one word, pathetic. But then have you ever been shown by your coach or teacher the correct way of loosening your muscles, relaxing your whole body while getting it warmed up and ready to cope with stress? I doubt it.

The Head   This is the logical place to begin. The moving joint of the head is the neck, and believe me, this is a very important part of the body.

You are required to head a ball, to connect your head with a ball that is travelling at somewhere between forty and sixty

71

miles an hour. When your forehead connects with the ball, the chances are that there is no ground beneath your feet. You are in mid-air, with no solid balance – no means of balance. So your body must absorb the stress of punching the ball with your forehead – more often than not punching the ball in a different direction from whence it came. The force of the impact immediately goes through the skull, down into the neck. Some of the force will be dispersed down to the back, as far as the waist. But the brunt of that force must be borne by your neck.

Another stress situation for the neck is when a challenging opponent puts the full force of his arm across your neck – possibly between 12 and 14 stone of defender behind an arm or elbow. Your neck had better be capable of taking that kind of punishment, or you are in big trouble.

To warm up the neck, simply rotate the neck as far as you can in an arc around the shoulders. Do this from right to left, then from left to right. You will soon feel the neck beginning to loosen up.

I should add here that this exercise is not just for footballers. There is no reason why people who have nothing to do with sport should not do it and the following exercises every day. The added advantage is that older people can do them without exerting any strain on their heart, so long as they feel comfortable while exercising. Common sense must always be applied.

In this exercise for the head, and for all the following exercises that appertain to the waist and upwards of the body, always stand with feet apart and well planted on the ground. This gives better balance.

The Shoulders The next moving joints are the shoulders. I begin exercising them by attempting to 'walk' my hands in the air, gradually extending the stride as far as possible, using head and shoulders in co-ordination. The arms must be kept straight. The head should be moving backwards and forwards as the hands punch the air. Try to get the arms as far behind the head as possible every time you punch.

Next, put both arms straight out in front of you, then pull them back as far as possible in a sideways arc, sticking out your chest and pushing your head forward.

Then, extending your arms sideways at shoulder height, swivel from the waist to bring one arm as far behind you as possible, looking straight along the arm all the time. Repeat the exercise with the other arm.

To achieve a really supple movement in the shoulders and back, lean forward at the waist, arms bent, and literally box yourself, rolling your shoulders in as large circles as possible.

The armpits and sides　The armpits can, obviously, be tied in with the shoulders. But nevertheless, they must not be overlooked. They have to be extended, warmed up and relaxed just like the other important body areas.

Keeping your legs spread apart, lift your right arm over your head, then, bending as far as possible at the waist to the left, stretch the arm as far as possible over your head and past your shoulder. When you have stretched your right arm, repeat the exercise using the other arm, and leaning as far as you can to the right. Now rest your hands on your hips and lean right, then left in a similar fashion. With legs still apart, keep both hands on hips and bend the upper half of your body around in a gentle, rolling movement so that at one stage of the roll, you are staring down past your knees, and at the opposite stage, you are staring at the sky. Remember, though, that during this, or any other exercise, you never jerk your body. Allow your body to flow smoothly at all times.

Upper body and hamstrings　We have already done a power of good to the upper body while exercising the neck, shoulders, armpits and waist. The next exercise requires the feet to be spread well apart, the legs as straight as possible.

Let the trunk simply hang down as far it will go. But do not jerk down. Let your trunk stretch down, slowly and steadily. Before long you will feel your hamstrings working, stretching and adjusting to the exercise. Do not fear damaging yourself.

73

WIN!

It is a physical impossibility for you to work, during good balances, against your own body, and pull a muscle. Your brain will always tell you when to stop. Only when outside influences come into contact with your body will injury occur – by 'outside influences' I mean kicking a ball, tackling an opponent, slipping over in mud or on ice and so on. When you are working against your own body-weight, your brain is the safety valve, the best safety valve in the business. When you stretch and stretch, you can guarantee that at some stage of the exercise, your brain will tell you to stop, and stop you will. However, it is important to remember that if you have not previously done much exercising, you must be very gradual in your increase of stress and demands upon your own body.

The groins Standing with your legs as far apart as possible, put your trunk weight over your left leg, and allow that weight to bend your leg down so that your bottom is as near to your heel as possible, all the time keeping your right leg stretched out to the side, again as far as possible. Hold it there for a few seconds, feeling your right groin stretching. Repeat the exercise on the other leg. Now, as Bobby Robson says: 'Invert it.' I am not too sure what he means by that, but the principle is the same. Put your weight on your left leg, foot planted firmly on the ground, and this time stretch your other leg out behind you. Again, wait a few seconds, feel the groin stretching, then repeat the exercise on the other leg. Again, allow your body-weight to take you down slowly to a position where your bottom is attempting to touch your heel. If you can make contact then you have certainly never had a cartilage operation!

This is one exercise where it is vitally important not to jerk because a groin is a very flimsy piece of muscle – yet it has to take the whole of your trunk-weight and that weight is passed through the groin, into the leg. That's a lot of weight to be carried.

The hamstrings Stand upright to attention, then let your trunk slowly go forward until you touch your toes. If your

74

elbows touch your toes then you are either double-jointed or possess incredibly short legs! I must repeat the warning about jerking through exercises. By the time you have finished reading this chapter, 'Don't jerk through any exercise' will be branded on your memory – which will be all to the good.

The one difference between this exercise and the exercise concerning upper body and hamstrings is that this one requires the legs to be together.

Thighs, knees, ankles   How about the front of the thighs? A big muscle, a strap, goes down the front of the thighs. This is the kicking muscle. It is the muscle that pulls the lower part of the leg from the bent to the straight position, which is the kicking movement. If you attempt to kick a ball before you have warmed up this muscle, it can tear and tear very nastily, anywhere between the knee and the hip.

Stand as straight as possible, feet together, raise one foot behind you, grab hold of the top of the foot and gently pull your heel towards your bottom. Give it a nice gentle pull, then repeat the exercise with the other leg.

For the knees, get hold of something firm enough to take your weight, then slowly descend into a position where you are squatting with your bottom on your heels. Keep your feet flat on the floor so your bottom is attempting to descend to the level of the heels.

The best ankle exercise involves raising a foot off the floor, and rotating it in as wide an arc as possible on the ankle joint. Do this for a few seconds, then repeat the exercise with the other foot.

There are variations to most exercises. But I believe that the exercises I have listed in this chapter will enable you to warm up the vital parts of your body that require warming, before you begin a training session or a match. Having done these exercises, you can then turn to the more strenuous, jerking movements such as star-jumps, astride jumps, jumping to bring knees to chest, jumping to head an imaginary ball, high-kicking, running on the spot and sprinting on the spot. Such exercises are often done first. *This is wrong.* The body must be warmed up and relaxed before it can be jerked about.

Once you are out on the pitch, you should make full use of the pre-match warm-up time. You should do a few stretches, as described, followed by long-striding runs, building them up gradually until you are sprinting flat-out. This takes very little time to complete. But once they are done, you will have that vital extra confidence when the match begins.

If you stick to a regular warm-up routine, you will reduce the chances of pulling a muscle, straining a joint or damaging that complex computer on which your future as a professional footballer depends. As I said earlier, there is little or nothing you can do to avoid the everyday knocks and bumps you will receive while you are playing. But as long as you are properly prepared beforehand, your body will absorb far more stress than if you go out and attempt to warm up by running flat-out from the whistle. Having the confidence in your body to put it through a tough, testing time is one of the key factors in your career as a professional footballer.

SIX
The Importance of Diet

I was half-way through my pile of mash, beans, fried eggs and fried tomatoes when I noticed the horrified expressions on the faces of two supporters nearby. They did not have to say anything. I knew what was coming. Sure enough, one of them could not resist the temptation.

'You should be eating steak before a game, not all that fattening stodge,' he said. 'Footballers are supposed to keep fit. What are you doing tucking into that lot the day before a big match?'

Grinning foolishly, my mouth crammed with potato, I shrugged my shoulders. There was no point in my attempting to explain. It takes too long. And anyway, I get tired of going through the reasons behind my 'diet' with every outraged fan who assumes I am a glutton. So I ordered a large piece of gateau, and put two heaped teaspoons of sugar into my tea.

However, the importance of diet to the young footballer is paramount. There are old wives' tales to be swept away, myths to be shattered. Diet is every bit as important as training, coaching and discipline to the professional.

There are two diets – one for the sportsman and one for the layman. The sportsman's diet must be geared to his physical requirements. The layman's diet is constructed on the basis of providing the body with fuel, filling the empty stomach and adding an extra dimension to social occasions.

The exercises I listed in the previous chapter can be done by sportsmen and laymen. Both will benefit, neither will suffer. The sportsman *must* do the exercises, the layman *may* do them if he wants to keep his body reasonably fit, supple and alert. But whereas the exercises suit both parties, the subject of diet takes the sportsman and the layman down very different paths. To hammer home the point, the footballer's diet is exactly the opposite of that of the layman.

A footballer who completes his game on Saturday with the knowledge that he does not have another game until the next Saturday bases his diet accordingly. But his diet for that week would be different if he had another match on the Tuesday or Wednesday night. Let us assume that you have played on Saturday, and do not have a match until next Saturday. Your intake for the week should consist mainly of a simple protein diet until about mid-day Thursday, and a concentrated carbohydrate diet from Thursday evening up to the kick-off.

If that formula sounds either severe or extreme, allow me to go back a few years, back to the origins of a diet system that has proved a great help to me in my career. During the early part of my stay with Newcastle I discovered that when I sweat, whether in training or while playing, I lose iron from my body as well as body-salt. For many years I was unaware of this fact, and put my feelings of sluggishness down to an incorrect diet or a lack of energy. Once the doctor had diagnosed my problem, I settled down to a diet that included lots of greens and 'blacks' – cabbage, cress, cauliflower and. the occasional bottle of Guinness – food containing iron as the basic compound. I was also instructed to report back to the doctor every two months for what proved to be extremely uncomfortable injections which replaced the lost iron not replaced by this diet.

About the same time as I was having these 'jabs' I became fascinated with the unusual diet of my team-mate Frank Clark, because while I was nibbling away at non-fattening meals, piled high with greens, Frank tucked into mountains of potatoes, bread, ice cream, cake and bars of chocolate! Finally, my patience and curiosity went in opposite directions. I tackled Frank about his diet, and he explained the formula. I was doubly impressed when I discovered that

Frank is a qualified laboratory technician as well as a damn good full-back. We discussed myths and old wives' tales that dominate teachings on diet. We discovered that some of the beliefs date back to the last century.

Bill Shankly – during his heyday as manager of Liverpool – is an example of someone who had a strange match-day ritual regarding diet. He insisted that his players ate burnt steak before every game! Yes, mad but true. Shankly used to wander into the kitchen to watch the steaks being murdered, just to ensure that they were sufficiently 'tanned' before they were served. His logic? Shankly had eaten burnt steaks before playing during his pre-war days as a Preston North End star. And he said: 'If it was good for me, then it's good enough for you!'

I adopted Frank's formula, studied it deeply, read books on the subject of body requirements and discovered that there is a wealth of information, invaluable to professional footballers, that they do *not* have at their finger-tips.

Returning to your diet, I will deal first with the protein aspect. The human body requires the same amount of protein every week. It makes no difference whether you are lying in bed, asleep, or running flat-out in an exhausting athletic event. The body will use up the same amount of protein no matter what. It does not burn up protein in the same way as it does carbohydrates. We are all meat, fish and/or dairy produce eaters – foods from which most protein supplied to the body is extracted. So the supply is as constant as its use.

However, you must not eat protein foods without some carbohydrates. You must maintain a balance in your diet. A few potatoes with your meat and greens are fine. It is essential that the body be supplied with a regular amount of iron and vitamins. But by the time you reach Thursday evening, your diet changes dramatically. Now you begin your carbohydrate intake on a big scale, always remembering that the same maxim applies: maintain a balance in diet. The body converts carbohydrate to blood-sugar, which in turn provides the body with energy. You must eat bread, potatoes, pasta, jam, chocolate, sweets, cake and biscuits – just about

79

as fattening a collection as you can imagine. You will require a little time to establish exactly how much energy you require: there is no point in over-eating to the extent of providing the body with more blood-sugar than it needs. This is where the problems can set in. Unwanted energy, the energy that may not be used up, converts to fat after about three days.

It also helps to know which of the carbohydrate foods convert quicker than others. Jam, for instance, converts to blood-sugar in about four to five hours. So you can eat jam on the morning of the match, knowing that by the time you go out to play the jam will have become fuel for the testing ninety minutes ahead.

My breakfast on a match-day comprises cornflakes and peach juice. Cornflakes contain a salt-like compound that prevents cramp. Peach juice converts very quickly to blood-sugar. Just before a match I eat toast and jam and a bar of chocolate to add a final, energy-giving top-up to my body. By the time I reach the last ten or fifteen minutes, that extra energy may mean the difference between winning and losing. You will establish your own exact routine after trial and a little worthwhile error. Once you know what your body requires in the way of blood-sugar, you can work out your diet accordingly.

I cannot over-emphasise the importance of your diet. Some lads are prone to putting on weight just by walking past a fish-and-chip shop. Others could eat the shop out of chips and never gain an ounce. This is all to do with metabolism and how quickly the body burns up blood-sugar. A quick-burner will stay lean and trim. A slow-burner will always have to guard against those extra few pounds of weight.

If you ask a doctor for the best method of losing weight, the chances are he will advise you to eat a little at a time, but eat often. This is because the stomach is the culprit, not the whole body. Over-eating causes the stomach to enlarge. So it becomes accustomed to being filled on demand. So when hunger-pangs begin, it is the stomach demanding the food. The body does not require so much.

1 Those formative years. Macdonald (extreme right, front row) lines up with his school team

2 An early example of the Macdonald 'long throw'

3 A career is born. Macdonald scores his first League goal in a mid-week match against Crystal Palace

The shirts are different but the style is unmistakable. 4 (*above*) Macdonald gets in a shot against Queen's Park Rangers during his final season with Newcastle United. 5 (*below*) Leeds and England star Tony Currie, one of the players Macdonald advises young players to watch, can't prevent the author from getting in a shot

Memorable moments playing for England at Wembley. 6 (*above*) Macdonald ignores the acrobatic efforts of the Cyprus centre-half to head the fourth of his five goals in a record-equalling 5–0 win. 7 (*below*) World champions West Germany are beaten. Macdonald gets on the end of Alan Ball's right wing cross to head England's second goal in a 2–0 win

Four players from the auth...
list of 'men to watch'

8 Leicester centre-forw...
Frank Worthington v...
combines skill and elega...
with powerful shooting, esp...
ally with his left foot

9 England and QPR win...
Dave Thomas, seen fir...
Rangers into the lead agai...
Wolves. Thomas is one of...
best crossers of a ball in...
League

10 Southampton's Mike Channon, who is one of the most effective players at running off the ball. He is also pretty useful on the ball, as he shows in this picture of a match against Stoke at The Dell

11 Denis Law, one of the all-time 'greats' and a player Macdonald watched as often as possible. He combined exciting skills and flair with a fiery temperament and passion Here exceptional balance enables him to waltz around a helpless goalkeeper

The two sides of being a pro. 12 (*above*) Macdonald encourages three
Arsenal fourth team players to question him and each other in a football
discussion before training. 13 (*opposite above*) The time for talking is over.
The author dives in between surprised Coventry defenders to head a
spectacular goal at Highbury

As expected, the game against Newcastle described in Chapter 14: 'A Day in the Life', is hotly contested. 14 (*opposite below*) Two Newcastle defenders make sure their former team-mate does not reach the penalty area. 15 (*below*) Once a pal, always a pal. Macdonald and Newcastle goalkeeper Mick Mahoney share a joke, despite the obvious pressures on both players

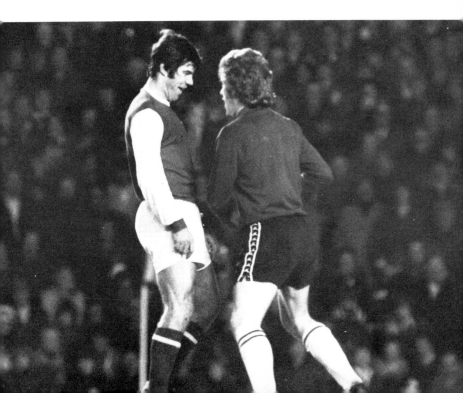

16 A blast from the past! Macdonald clearly sees the funny side of Geoff Nulty's yelled instructions. Three goals prove that words were just not enough on the day

17 What a fantastic feeling. The author receives the congratulations of his Arsenal team-mates after scoring the first of his three goals. Left to right: Trevor Ross, Frank Stapleton, Malcolm Macdonald, Alan Ball and Pat Howard

By eating a reasonable amount of food at regular intervals during the day, you can supply your body with all the necessary protein, carbohydrate, iron and vitamins without packing out the stomach with one massive load. Slowly but surely, the stomach will return to its normal size and the demands for food will diminish.

Mastication is another vital aspect of diet. Too many people bolt their food, swallowing half-chewed portions of food that the stomach has to handle. Unless food is chewed over and over until it is almost pulp the stomach is left with the responsibility of converting solids, and this leads to a traffic jam just below the base of the rib-cage. Apart from the problems of indigestion, stomach pains and heart-burn, you will begin to notice your weight going up – not because you are over-eating, but because you are under-masticating. The stomach will not be able to convert the near-solids as quickly as it would convert properly masticated food, and the dispersion of the various essentials to the system is slowed up. With the stomach doing the job that should have been done by the jaws, excess pressure is exerted on the heart, which can lead to problems in later life. You should masticate each mouthful of food about fifty times.

So, time for a quick re-cap. Your diet after match-day begins on a protein base until Thursday evening, then moves on to building up an energy store for the next match on a carbohydrate base. Remember to include some carbohydrate with the protein and *vice versa*.

If you are playing a match on Tuesday, you still eat a protein-based meal after playing, eat protein on Sunday but again follow this with a two-day build-up of carbohydrates. This is very important.

During your professional career, you will encounter various difficulties concerning food and drink; if you are unable to come to terms with them they may grow out of all proportion and seriously affect your career. It is vitally important to have a solid base from which to work. Organisation in your life will give you strength and a measure of peace of mind. You may find one particular rhythm of life more comfortable than another, so stick to that life-style as it will create a better balance of mind.

When you notice that you are either over-weight or under-weight, you can tackle the situation without experiencing a sense of panic from within. Providing you are properly armed with knowledge about your own body, there is no reason to worry.

If there is one well-worn old saying that I would like to see deleted from the English language it's that misleading, problem-causing nonsense: 'Ignorance is bliss.' It is nothing of the kind. Ignorance usually leads to unhappiness, insecurity, anxiety and countless problems.

I advise you to begin examining your diet as soon as possible. It has an immense bearing on your career, your health and your state of mind – on and off the football field.

SEVEN

The Fans

The fork, laden with spaghetti, was mid-way between my plate and mouth when a beefy hand smashed down on my wrist. An autograph book plopped on the table. 'Sign that for my son,' was the curt instruction.

Immediately, my natural defence mechanism switched on. I just ignored the interruption and lifted the fork of spaghetti mouthwards. Down came the beefy hand, this time with a violent grip. 'I said, sign that book for my son.'

In a matter of seconds, a whole series of pictures flashed through my mind. Returning home from training that morning, arranging a baby-sitter for the night, showering, dressing and driving my wife, Julie, out to dinner. Here we were, enjoying a quiet evening out together, chatting about our new house, our children's new school and, we thought, relaxing in total anonymity. No such luck.

I glanced at Julie across the table. She stifled a grin. Another wife might have looked petrified, embarrassed or angry. But Julie has been through this little one-act drama many times. Often, her reaction becomes my strength.

I refused to look up. By now, the character standing by my left shoulder was shuffling his feet, growing more self-conscious by the second. By now, the people at the tables around us were staring at him. Not at me, at him. And he knew it.

My third attempt at lifting the fork met with another mid-air interception. This time the beefy hand almost pushed me face-down into the plate. 'Are you going to sign that book?'

With a deft flick of the right hand on the tip of the laden fork in my left hand, I propelled a dollop of spaghetti through the air. It landed on his jacket. For a tense moment he had the option of throwing a punch in the direction of my head or backing off into the shadows. He glared, swore under his breath and backed off. I politely asked him if he would like his unsigned book back.

Having set out to make me look small and himself the tough guy, the autograph hunter finished up looking a fool. Yet had he walked up to our table, quietly made his apologies for interrupting our meal and asked for my autograph, I would have signed with pleasure ... asking for his son's name so I could add a little message.

Sometimes a conversation develops. The interlude is pleasant and everyone is happy. There is no need for the brutal, ignorant approach. You will experience similar 'attacks' on your privacy. What matters is how you handle them.

How easy it would have been to have played the outraged citizen. Angry words exchanged, arms waving around menacingly, the whole atmosphere spoiled for countless people.

I have learned that the only way to handle such characters is to turn their rudeness back in their direction. Show them up for the bores they are. What you must never do is either lose your temper or create a scene. You are the person who will suffer as a result of any unpleasant incident.

This chapter is about football fans. It may seem harsh that I have opened the chapter with a disagreeable incident. But there is a comparison to be made. The contrast in personalities is astonishing. You will meet them all.

Some weeks after the incident at the dinner table, I opened a letter and found a crumpled pound note attached to a short message. It read: 'Arsenal are the greatest team in the world. Please buy all the players a drink from me.'

The 'author' of that letter was a little lad of thirteen. He probably spent all his pocket money for the week in that lovely gesture. I was speechless. But I knew I could not send the money back. That would have been churlish and ungracious. He may have only been thirteen, but he would have seen through any attempt to 'reject' his offer.

I still have that pound at home. I told the players, who immediately recounted tales of similar gifts from fans – young and old. They send birthday cards, Christmas cards, locks of hair, photographs and little presents.

Footballers are basically warm-hearted lads who appreciate the sentiments behind such gifts. If only every weekday were twenty hours longer, we would give our thanks personally, as is so often requested. It is impossible for players to meet every fan who writes; but that is not to say we don't reply to their letters, or appreciate them.

So you see what I mean by contrasts. Professional footballers must be prepared to meet and deal with every type of human being. Knowing how to meet people is vitally important. That is why you must be educated as a public relations officer on behalf of yourself, your club and your profession.

Everything you are taught must be based on the premise that you and everybody else are human beings with feelings, emotions, fears, hopes and dreams. Where one player might be capable of handling a tricky situation in public, you might retreat into a shell or lose your temper in the heat of the moment and risk acquiring a reputation as a hothead.

It is so easy for a perfectly well-behaved young lad to be branded as a trouble-maker. All he has to do is go to a club or pub with his pals after a match, order a lager and then get embroiled in a stupid argument with a half-drunk customer. The next day he discovers that he is considered a lush, a boozer, a night-club brawler. Such a reputation takes a few minutes to acquire and most of a career to lose. I believe young footballers need a gradual, full education about the facts of football life. Instinct will tell you when the fans love you and when they are not very impressed with your form. Football fans are quick to voice their opinions from the terraces. However, when you walk off the pitch, you must expect those same fans to voice those same opinions if and when they see you.

Young players are often bewildered when confronted, in a hotel foyer, outside a ground or on a train, by a group of fans determined to air their views. Avoid arguments. Avoid the temptation to encourage a conversation that looks as if it could become heated. Young players expect reaction from the fans when they're doing their job – playing football. But often players are unable to come to terms with criticism when it is levelled at them when they are wearing their three-piece suits for the benefit of their girl-friends. No young man enjoys being cornered when his girl-friend is present. On such occasions, he must be able to handle a tricky situation and come away quickly and unscathed. I am not saying that every time a player meets football fans he is in for a row. Far from it. But I believe that it is the troublesome fans who must be guarded against.

Sometimes, it all boils down to whether or not you like people and enjoy their company. I love a good chat. I enjoy meeting fans no matter where they pop up – providing they are polite. Even then, funny things can happen. Two incidents come to mind.

I was sitting in a hotel foyer with some of the Newcastle players, waiting for the team-coach to collect us. Suddenly, I noticed a group of supporters across the hall, huddling around and exchanging words and looks. Instinct told me what to expect. Sure enough, out of the group stalked a very intense-looking young man clutching a photograph of the Newcastle team. 'I want you to sign that,' he said, thrusting the photo under my nose.

I looked at him, looked past him to the group of lads in the corner, then back to him again. Now he was red in the face and getting angry. 'Come on, sign it, will you.' He looked over his shoulder and tried to grin. I signed the photo and handed it back. Why? Because he had not intended to be rude. In fact the lad was nervous and embarrassed. His mates had thrown down the challenge: 'Go over and get Macdonald's autograph.' He had saved face.

When I had signed, he relaxed. It was as if he had been released from a vice-like grip of nerves. He mumbled: 'Thanks, thanks very much.' Suddenly, he turned on his heel and marched back towards his mates, chest out, photo under his arm. I understood that the whole incident was a terrifying ordeal for him. He felt embarrassed and ill-at-ease. But he refused to allow his fear to overcome him. I admired his guts. He may have appeared rude in his attitude, but in fact he was scared of a rebuke in front of his mates. It is important to know and appreciate the difference between rudeness and embarrassment. When you understand the difference, you will discover that nobody can corner you or catch you off guard through their behaviour, especially in public. You must always be on top and always remain cool. You are the public figure, and must expect to be under scrutiny from unseen eyes at all times.

Another day, a tall, lean, student character battled across a crowded room with a menu and flashed me a toothy grin. He asked me, very politely, to sign the menu twice, once for himself and once for his girl-friend. As I signed, he leaned over my shoulder to watch, tipping the beer glass in his left hand forwards until I felt a cold trickle on my leg. I looked down at my new trousers, looked up at him ... and he grinned, went pink and stared back at the half-signed menu, not realising where his beer was going. I continued signing as the trickle became a mini-flood, but still he didn't realise. I looked straight at him and down at the soggy pants, but he gave a nervous twitch, grabbed the menu and said, 'Awfully nice of you, thanks a lot.' I had to make a special effort to reply, 'It's my pleasure.' To me that is an amusing memory. If I meet that young man again, we can share a laugh – and the laundry bill.

The subject of fans has a very serious and worrying side. Everyone knows that most supporters are well-behaved citizens – people who buy a season ticket or who pay at the turnstile to follow their team. But there exists a minority of mindless idiots who tar football with a dirty brush: the yobs, the trouble-makers, who wear the colours of their club as they indulge in their bullying, brawling, swearing and wrecking.

These people must realise that the players they say they support detest them and everything they stand for. We have neither time nor sympathy for the rubbish of the football terraces.

I am all for stricter measures. The sooner these people are barred from football grounds, the sooner people will begin to bring their wives and youngsters back to the terraces.

It sickens me to pick up a Sunday paper and see the faces of the mindless waving their fists around the terraces. Because they are destroying the image of the club they say they support; because they detract from all that is so good and exciting about football fans in full voice; because they detract from the publicity that should be given to matches and to young players. Young players, who should be the centre of attention, are often relegated to down-page paragraphs – if they are lucky – because the idiots have once again grabbed the headlines.

Football fans are not all about hooliganism. I have met countless who remain in my memory for their humour, their kindness and their encouragement. Without them football would die. Equally, unless the idiots are swept away, football, as a spectator sport, is in danger of being seriously damaged.

My message to you is simple and direct. Never become involved with the idiot fringe. Never be drawn into situations where you become identified with them – on or off the field. It is so easy to nod in token agreement when a loud-mouth criticises a team-mate. Often, the young player does not hear exactly what has been said. But to get away quickly, he says: 'Yes, sure,' and pushes towards his escape. Before he has reached the team-coach, the word has got around that he has publicly criticised a colleague – fuel to the flames if the knockers have their knives out for a certain player.

Very often, groups of people make very tempting offers and invitations to attend parties or functions. It is equally tempting to say 'yes' without sufficient thought. Never agree to something without first making sure of all the facts, and, indeed, without making sure that you are free to attend. To agree to attend a function and then not turn up – either through forgetting or being otherwise engaged – leads to bad feeling and the rapid development of a bad reputation.

Fans are important. Every fan you meet is important. Without them, the professional game would not exist. But that is not to say that they own the players they follow. You must be polite – and demand a measure of civility in return. You must acknowledge the right of the fan to be critical, but never tolerate abuse. You must appreciate that your every word is cherished by some, and may be used as ammunition by others.

You represent your club on and off the pitch. But you also have a right to privacy, a social life and time to relax. It is simple to strike up a balance. There is no need to go to extremes. Club blazers do not have to be worn to bed, while it is important to remember that match days merit a shave, a spruce-up and a presentable appearance. Alec Stock always hammered home the same point: 'If you can play, then look as if you can play.'

Sometimes it is possible to bluff your way out of daft situations. Again, I emphasise the need for you to be calm and aloof at all times. I made a mistake at a disco one night and I have never forgotten it.

With a few team-mates on tour, I watched a group of locals dancing in the middle of the floor. One of them, a massive farmer-type character with bulging muscles and 6-foot-three inch frame, was giving a passable impersonation of an elephant with indigestion. Unable to hold back, I suddenly laughed. The performer glared up, stopped dancing and marched over to where I was standing.

'You're laughing at me, aren't you?' he growled. By now, his mates had gathered around. I shrugged my shoulders and accepted that I had been caught. I owned up. Up went his sleeves as I quickly eyed around for the nearest exit. Realising that I was cornered, I jumped up and put the index finger of my right hand on the side of his neck. 'One move and you're dead,' I snapped. His face drained of blood. One of my team-mates, seeing a way out of World War III, joined in: 'Do as he says, pal. He is an oriental master.'

The place was silent. I felt a complete fool standing there with my finger pressed into this character's neck. But I knew that if I budged, he would propel me through the wall.

The bluff seemed to last a lifetime before he mumbled: 'I don't like being laughed at, that's all. Next time ...' And the farmers and footballers joined forces to have a marvellous night together.

That could have developed into a terrible situation. But we kept our heads and stayed calm. Always remember that there is an alternative to fists.

Another change of climate. During your playing career, you will experience the wrath of the fans. If you are going through a lean spell or the team is struggling, you will, at some stage, go through the mill. It is important that you are prepared for this and that you know how quickly such situations can change. Hero today, villain next Saturday, or *vice versa*. Never allow your head to drop. Battle away, want the ball, don't hide or shirk your responsibilities. Yes, if you see a lot of the ball at a time when you are not playing well, you will be more noticeable every time you make a mistake. There is one way to beat the boo-boys – beat them with your ability. Your manager and team-mates are the best judges, not the knockers. I would rather have in my team an out-of-form player with guts and character than a highly-skilled mouse.

Be aware of what a team-mate is suffering if he is the butt of the crowd's frustration. By that I mean help him. Don't make his job more difficult. Never make gestures of frustration when he makes a mistake. You will only stoke up the crowd's anger, and they will continue to direct their anger at the same player. Encourage a player who is off form, especially when you hear the criticism-level from the terraces getting louder, more intense. Keep his head up. Battle to make him favourite to receive passes. Put yourself out a little bit to ensure that when you pass the ball to him, he has every chance of collecting it. One day you will be very grateful if someone does the same for you.

Never forget, however, that the apparent hatred directed at you when you are playing away from home is a source of strength – yes, strength. Because the more a crowd howl at you, the more they fear you. When the fans begin to bay, this is the time to be arrogant, be great, be positive in everything you do on the fields because the hatred between 3.00 p.m. and 4.45 p.m. becomes something entirely different when those same fans leave the ground and head for their local pub. Their conversation makes you realise that what was hatred matures to admiration and respect.

Remember, you are living out the dreams and fantasies of the fans on the terraces. When you miss a sitter or drop the ball over your own line, the crowd experiences the whole spectrum of disappointment, frustration and anger. When you score the winning goal or make the save of the match, your celebrations, no matter how extrovert they may be, will never match the fantastic reaction of your fans. They make the atmosphere. They *are* the atmosphere.

There are two ways of viewing a career as a professional footballer. You may look on the whole experience as a tough life spent within the pressure-cooker confines of a goldfish bowl. Or you may take the positive attitude and accept the pressure as part of a fantastic way to live.

There is one aspect of public life that you must learn about: public speaking. During your career, especially the successful periods, you will be invited to attend functions, open fêtes, present awards and make after-dinner speeches. At some stage, as early as possible, you must be taken aside and have all the terrors of public speaking explained. The whole ordeal – and the first after-dinner speech is always an ordeal – requires a little pre-thought and absolutely no panic.

People always want speakers to do well. Nobody wishes you to fall flat on your face. Even if you tell the worst joke ever told, people will laugh. Because they want to laugh, they want to be amused. Just don't bore them.

Presenting or being presented with an award are the two

easiest situations to cope with. Because no matter how badly you mumble your way through, the audience will roar their approval.

I have always maintained that a bit of the old attacking play goes down well at dinners. People like to share jokes as well as hear them. Very few audiences get upset if you have a little go in their direction.

For example, I was speaking at a mixed dinner one evening when a loud, female voice screeched out from a table over in the corner. 'Mr Macdonald, is it true that you can run faster than anybody else? I mean I saw you on "Superstars" and you ran ever so fast and I wonder if you can still run that fast ...' Yes, it was painful.

My reply was short but effective. 'Madam, if you were in pursuit, I would smash all Olympic sprint records.' She loved every minute of it. Everyone did.

On such occasions most people love to hear the kind of stories that happen behind the footballing scenes but are rarely publicized. Remember those amusing little incidents that happen in the dressing-room, during training or during and after matches – the incidents involving team-mates. Never 'tell tales out of school' or let down your professional colleagues, but do entertain people with an amusing, true story. They always enjoy it – particularly if they can identify with the characters.

When you boil everything down to its true level, you discover that the fans, the public, only want the same things you want – success, to win, to be associated with glory and triumph. I believe we can share these precious experiences – we players and fans.

EIGHT

The Press

I was shattered. A game we should have won had almost been lost. I was happy that we had fought back to draw with Birmingham. But I was far from happy with my own performance.

Most of the lads were laughing and joking, ribbing each other about 'missed sitters' and arguing as to whether or not the referee had been correct to award a penalty against David O'Leary. I sat in a corner worrying and wondering about the next day's newspaper headlines.

My problem was how to come to terms with what the sports reporters wanted to hear and what I wanted to say. I had scored a hat-trick in our 3–3 draw at St Andrews – and two of my goals coming late in the game with Birmingham 3–1 ahead. Instant hero!

Unfortunately life, and certainly football, is never as easy or as cut and dried as that. I did not feel I had any right to consider myself Arsenal's hero. What the press and public believe to be 'having a good game' or 'having a nightmare match' rarely matches the thoughts and feelings of the professional footballers they are judging.

As Arsenal's centre-forward, I had done a good job in so far as I had scored three goals. On the face of it, what more can be expected of a striker? And how easy it would have been to storm through the door and hold court, surrounded by reporters.

'Yes, I've worked hard on that move for weeks ... We hammered them out of sight ... I feel on top of the world ...

City couldn't hold me tonight ...' Yet those words would have screamed 'hypocrite' at me from every national newspaper the next morning.

The fact is I had played badly, and yet again we had let in too many goals. No doubt the Arsenal supporters who made the trip were delighted with our comeback, our three goals and a point. But as a professional I knew that my overall contribution had not come up to scratch. And my Arsenal team-mates knew it also.

Technically I was poor: my positioning, my reading of situations, my passing, my share of the spade-work. I had four chances, fluffed one and accepted three. But without those goals I would have stuck out like an ice-cream seller in the Sahara Desert.

The moment of truth arrives when the professional foot-baller comes face to face with the professional sports reporter. The confrontation is rarely balanced because usually there are a number of reporters surrounding one player who really only wants a beer and a calming half-hour.

Always, I hope for something original – a question that merits thought and a constructive answer. After this match I had already made up my mind to risk the backlash and say exactly how I felt. I might have known!

Hands thrust deep in trouser pockets, I wandered into the group of milling reporters, autograph hunters and back-slappers. That dreaded first question hit me between the eyes: 'Well Mal, how do you feel?' Now that took a lot of imagination. Resisting the temptation to reply: 'With my hands,' I made the best of another bad session. You might think I was being interviewed by a cub reporter, but I was trying to convey my feelings to one of Fleet Street's national newspaper representatives.

I explained that I was disappointed with my performance, and detailed exactly why, then made the point that while scoring goals is my job above all else, there is still that important 'all else' to consider. I hoped to hit the same wave-length as those reporters. But most of them stood, nodding, writing and relying on one or two to ask all the questions.

The next day my words leered out at me implying: 'Macdonald must be different.' That was not the way it was meant to turn out. But I should have known better and stuck to the age-old rules of the game. By giving honest answers, I laid myself open to being portrayed as the big-head who always has to say something out of the ordinary; the ego-tripper who is not satisfied with scoring his hat-trick and admitting that he is delighted. The trouble was, I had not said what the reporters were expecting me to say. I was not 'over the moon' or 'on cloud nine'.

I am not setting out this stall as a knocking campaign or an anti-press chapter. But I do have strong feelings on the whole system of publicity, communications and public relations. Every reporter, editor, footballer and supporter is entitled to put his cigarette lighter to the corner of each page if he disagrees with me. That's democracy.

I have cited that incident at Birmingham purely as an example of the small but niggling frustrations which arise every Saturday from doing and feeling one thing and being persuaded to say another. It is not actual dishonesty – on either side of the fence – more a lack of understanding and a total lack of what the whole media should be about: communication.

I want to be fair – to journalists, footballers and readers alike. If my thoughts in this chapter appear too biased in any direction – no apologies. Don't expect me to change now. I do not anticipate any bricks hurled through my windows.

For every unprofessional journalist there is an unprofessional footballer. Every profession has its bad eggs, rotten apples, call them what you like. But unfortunately they cause trouble, upset people and leave a trail of unhappiness in their muddy, bloody wake.

I hope to provide young lads with as much information and advice as possible on how to work with the press – and love every minute of it. Reporters can make or break a footballer. But rarely can the reverse be said. For that reason, I believe it is important to know the pitfalls and the safe platforms when he sees them.

I remember talking to a Fourth Division manager who was bitterly upset about a report carried in a national newspaper. His team had spent most of the season struggling and the game in question ended with neither side having scored.

The manager did not deny that the match had been a poor spectacle, nor did he attempt to wriggle out of the fact that he was having a lean time; but he was close to tears of anger on reading one of the match reports and what it said about one of his young players.

'I've spent months building up the lad's confidence,' he explained, 'and he responded well. He's only seventeen and full of natural talent. But he's nervous, lacks a bit of drive and needs nursing along at this stage of his career.

'This reporter has watched our game, given us a hammering in his paper and predicted a gloomy future for me. I can take all of that. The reporter has his job to do and is entitled to give stick as well as praise.

'But he'll never know the damage he has done to that youngster. The lad came off hoping for a word of encouragement from me, and I gave it. His parents were watching what was only his third first-team game. He played a reasonable game. He made mistakes and was obviously influenced by the anxiety of the more senior players around him.

'But the reporter slaughtered him. By the time the lad had watched his parents reading the report, his confidence hit zero-level. I have to begin all over again.'

I can picture the scene. Sports editor sends reporter to cover Snurge Rovers *v* Hapless Rangers. Already the man on the job is consumed with apathy. He has difficulty parking his car. He can't find his seat and telephone plug in the ancient, windy press-box. The match begins and he is still fiddling around in the dark as fellow journalists mutter, 'Sit down for Christ's sake.' At half-time there is no tea. At full-time he can't even get a glass of beer.

By now the reporter has had one hell of an enjoyable night after doing a full day's work into the bargain. To make matters worse, he has watched two struggling teams thud and boot their way to a goal-less draw – a match with all the exciting, stimulating, controversial ingredients of a whist drive in a Bournemouth hotel.

At 9.30 p.m. the reporter is still sitting in that windy press-box writing his match report. Human nature rules. The reporter bears no actual malice. But he has had a rough and exhausting day and night. The match has bored him stiff. So he gives both teams some stick.

In the midst of all these contributing factors is the blossoming career of a young lad – crushed by a handful of ill-chosen criticisms.

A youngster making a similar debut or third appearance for Arsenal or Spurs would receive very different treatment. 'Showed lots of promise ... Needs experience but has what it takes ... Played well in very good-class company ...' You have read it all before.

But who cares a damn about that young lad of Snurge Rovers? Be bigger than that!

It is important that somebody takes the time and trouble to explain to you that a slating in the press is not the end of the world. In a young mind, full of ambition and desperate for encouragement, strong criticism of this nature can do nothing but harm if it is allowed to. Young players must be helped to realise that their future will be paved with days as the hero and days as the flop. They must appreciate that in the often fickle eyes of press and public alike, they will only be as good as their last game. We all are.

The press could help. If reporters took a few minutes to analyse situations such as the one I mentioned, they could provide a young player with a shot in the arm, bigger than anything his manager or parents could give. When a young player is full of confidence, it is easy to knock him down. But when he is down, it is a difficult job building him up again.

This brings me back to the problem of communication. I believe the time has come for footballers and journalists to begin educating each other. The gap between us is too great. Too many players tar reporters with the same brush. Too many reporters tar players with the same brush. The result is all too often negative, naive half-truths, rumours and myths.

I have sat with players and journalists discussing football, footballers and various aspects of the game – in confidence. 'Off the record' is the well-known phrase.

I have also picked up a newspaper the next day and read so-called confidences quoted in 'exclusive' stories, such as 'A player revealed to me ...'

Reporters have their job to do but I refuse to accept that they really believe a confidence is not exactly as it is described in the dictionary: 'A firm trust, imparting of private matters.'

There are journalists with whom I feel at ease and with whom I am prepared to discuss any aspect of football because I know I can rely on their integrity and honesty. A very good journalist friend once said to me: 'That point you made to me last week, can I use it now?' That is a good friend and a good professional.

Others, unfortunately, are not trustworthy. What amazes me is that these reporters cannot understand where they go wrong. Surely it stands to reason that no proper relationship can be established without honesty and integrity on both sides? The reporters I trust receive a hell of a lot more co-operation from me than those who attempt to stuff words down my throat.

I remember a First Division player who, good though he was at his job, had little to say or offer in the changing room. Players tended to ignore his occasional comments. The man was and is a damn good professional footballer. But he is also a slow-witted character.

As I said before, human nature rules. Imagine being in his position. (And this is where we, the players, are equally at fault.) He sits and listens, probably longing to contribute to our after-match discussion. Perhaps one point is eating him up. His frustration grows because he can't muster sufficient self-confidence to get in and say his piece. So out he goes, hair half-dried, doing up his tie and feeling at odds with everyone. Suddenly he is surrounded by reporters who ask: 'Are you worried about the defence? You've let in a lot of goals – should there be a change of goalkeeper or is it stemming from midfield? Are the forwards working hard enough to get back?'

For the first time in weeks, somebody wants to know how he feels. At last he has a platform, and a public platform at that. He gets everything out of his system.

Now for a change of tense. I saw this happen. I saw the player in question spilling his soul in public, saying the most astonishing things – not out of deliberate malice but as if he were releasing a valve. That same player could not believe his eyes the next day when he read some of the headlines. We were more to blame than any reporter. Because footballers should look ahead, think ahead. But unfortunately, headlines are not easily shared. I have no sympathy for experienced professionals who shoot off their mouths and then cry wolf when reporters report what they have been told.

Yes, I believe we footballers and reporters both need to take a long, hard look at our roles. Are reporters fair to players? Are players fair to reporters?

You may emerge from a changing-room after one of your first games at the top and be confronted by a group of eager reporters firing questions at you from all sides. If you have been properly advised, you will quickly assess every question and answer accordingly. What you must not do is say 'yes' or 'no' to any question, put to you in such a way that a one-word reply suffices. If a reporter asks you: 'Is your leg injured?' you can reply: 'Yes, I have pulled a muscle,' or 'No, it is just a bruise.' However, if the reporter asks: 'Is your muscle pulled, or do you think it might be something more serious like a hamstring or ligaments?' You must reply in full: 'There is no question of ligament trouble or hamstring trouble. My leg is bruised, nothing more.'

You will learn this the hard way. Once, when asked such a question, I replied: 'No, I'm fine.' Next day I read that I had limped away from the ground, hastily denying that I had developed ligament trouble. In a way, that report was accurate. I had limped a little and had denied having ligament trouble. But read it again and grab the

99

inference. On such small points are mountains of waffle built and rumours snowballed.

The situation is a pitfall in itself. Reporter and player get caught up in the routine, neither giving enough thought to the job or what it means.

What astonishes me is that there must be millions of words written about football in England, Ireland, Scotland and Wales every week. How? What do newspapers and magazines find to write about? Unrealistic copy demands to fill acres of space result in nonsense stories and waffle that serve to make football appear a complex game, shrouded in cloaks of mystery and suspense. The popular 'Bloggs to join Rovers' is a good case in point. Now Bloggs has probably never considered joining Rovers. But his wife reads the story and immediately grills Bloggs as to why she has to read about her husband's moves in newspapers. Mother-in-law rings up to ask daughter why she still can't keep Bloggs in line, and does she really intend moving house yet again? Bloggs' manager wants to know why Bloggs has not mentioned his intentions to his club. The chairman summons the manager to 'clear up' this business of Bloggs joining Rovers. Meanwhile, Rovers manager is hastily telling reporters that he wouldn't touch Bloggs with a barge-pole. And so the whole lunatic merry-go-round spins faster and faster. And what about poor Bloggs?

To the journalists who write stories without checking their facts or without caring who they hurt, I say – you are out of order.

To the footballers who provide reporters with gossip that simply is not true, I say – you are out of order.

Too many reporters stand back and wonder how to bridge the gap. They shy away from straightforward talking on man-to-man level. Too many players stand back and wonder how to handle the spotlight instead of giving honest answers and dismissing stupid questions.

We are all guilty of allowing what could be a fantastic relationship to develop into a phoney game of cliches, old-hat and waffle. Players are guilty of giving those well-worn replies to those well-worn questions. Reporters are guilty of assuming the public knows no better. Standards all round must go up or the whole system is in danger of collapse.

You will discover, as I discovered, that some reporters become your best pals, others your worst enemies. I have received invaluable help from the press during my career. Of that there is no doubt. There have been times when I have wanted to say something about a game or a person – something positive, a point of view. I have spoken to reporters and felt ten feet tall at the results. They have felt equally delighted with good copy and a big headline. You will meet such professionals during your career, men who are proud of their calling who are unafraid to sit in a press-box and give their honest opinion before facing the players they have written about.

I have never seen or heard of a professional footballer who found a bone to pick with Geoffrey Green of *The Times*. This man is different class. Not for him the proverbial and detestable 'after-match quotes' syndrome. Certainly, straight questions merit straight answers. But the prying, digging questions are the ones I detest.

Geoffrey prefers to wax lyrical about the good things he watched, the enjoyable aspects of the game, and the things that he disliked – and why. Never mind what Bloggs felt about the referee's eighty-ninth-minute row with Snoggins or how 'sick as a parrot' the manager felt about that 'goal that was definitely offside' or (that favourite word) 'diabolical'.

I appreciate that any journalist who picks up this book and reads this chapter will ask: 'Who the hell does this Macdonald think he is?' or: 'What right has Macdonald to question how we do our jobs?'

How would they feel, however, if I were to throw that question back at them?

I dislike being told how to do my job by laymen. I accept justified criticism: I have to. That is part of my way of life. But I draw the line at being told about football. Nothing angers me, or any professional footballer, more.

101

When I read some match reports, I cringe. It appears to me that some reporters describe the movements of the ball rather than the game and the men who play it. Maybe that is why a player who has touched the ball many times in a game will receive high marks, and the man who has run unselfishly for ninety minutes to create room for team-mates will be either ignored or described as having had a 'nightmare'.

Rarely, if ever, have I turned, arms aloft after scoring a goal, and not seen my name in the following day's newspapers as the scorer. But I wish I had a pound for every time I've read that Smith laid on the pass for the cross or Brown crossed the ball when I know he did not. The obvious is seen, but the nuances of the game are missed.

There is too much nonsense talked about football and the people involved in it. As if we don't have headaches, toothaches, children who keep us up all night or cars that refuse to start. Few reporters bother to find out why a player has looked like death warmed up during a game. The immediate reaction is: 'Too much of the bright lights and high living.' The fact that his wife is in hospital and he has a baby to worry about rarely hits the headlines. Footballers only bare their souls on the pitch, not their private lives.

Yes, we are just as much to blame for this daft cloak of secrecy. The standard reply 'No comment' is all that is needed to fire the imagination and the determination of any reporter worth his salt.

How much better it would be if clubs and players got the whole business in perspective. It is to the material benefit of football and the press to provide the public with accurate and reliable information on the game and those who take part in it. We need to clear the channels of information, that's all.

I sympathise with reporters who hit back by describing some of the antiquated press facilities we have in Britain, especially compared with abroad. I too dislike dancing around the Rolls-Royces in the rain. I hate huddling in a corner with the world trying to get by while reporters battle to meet their deadlines. There is nothing worse for any reporter than to stand around in the cold, forbidding confines of a club car-park, waiting for players to emerge from the bath.

As I said, both sides have lots to do. Especially if the likes of you, the reader, are to benefit from their relationship with the press – and *vice versa*.

My message is simple. Tell the truth and ignore duff, negative questions. Don't discuss your team-mates in anything other than general terms. Sure, say Fred had a good game or a bad game – but don't attack Fred's performance as an excuse for anything. Don't let down a fellow professional. Tell Fred what you think by all means – in the changing room and after the match.

If a reporter rings you and explains that he needs a story, either about you or about your team, don't slam down the phone. Think about the things you have done or are about to do in that week, make the effort to co-operate. Provide the reporter with a sensible story along whatever lines are genuinely available. He will probably have a reasonable line, anyway.

Good publicity is invaluable. Never forget that. Do not be afraid to say you loved every minute of a function you attended or a game you played. Be positive in all that you say. If all you can think of is something along negative lines, don't bother. There is too much already being said and written about what is supposed to be wrong with football.

I have made mistakes in my relationships with journalists over the years and I have learned by them. There was a time when I would bounce out of the changing room and fill their notebooks. I was young and still learning my trade.

You are learning your trade. You require assistance every step of the way. Which brings me back to that night in the Birmingham City changing room. If all that can be asked of any footballer at the end of a three-all draw in which he scored a hat-trick is: 'Well Mal, how do you feel?' then the system has some way to go before it is correct.

Football is a tough business as well as being the greatest

WIN!

game on earth. All I ask is that the whole pack of us –
players, managers, pressmen and the public – make it that bit
easier for you to make the grade. One and all should go out of
their way to make young players aware of the power and
influence of the written word. Educate young players to
choose those words – carefully and honestly.

NINE

Superstitions and Traditions

We piled off the coach with a sigh of relief. A series of guided tours around the streets of Liverpool had done nothing for the butterflies in our stomach and most of us could not resist cracking a wry joke as we filed past the embarrassed coach driver. Players begin to feel the flutters when they arrive in the town that houses their opponents for the day. Playing Liverpool on their own ground is extra-special. So driving around in circles, lost, with the ground visible over the roof-tops, is somewhat disconcerting.

By the time our driver had found the main entrance, we were twenty minutes late, and anxious to get into our dressing-room. As we walked down the players' corridor, I noticed a plaque of wood on the wall in front of us. The Liverpool crest was carved in the centre with the words 'This is' above the crest, and 'Anfield' below it.

'This is Anfield.' The Newcastle players looked at each other. We knew we were at Liverpool. So why were Liverpool making such a point of telling us where we were? Bill Shankly and Joe Harvey were standing below the plaque, doubtless exchanging colourful memories, so I decided to indulge in a little rib-jabbing. Pointing up at the plaque I said: 'There you are, Joe, I told you we were at the right place.' Shankly wheeled around on me and gravelled: 'You'll soon find out you're playing at the right place!' There was no mistaking the tone of his voice.

That was one in the eye for me. But later on, when I asked him why he put 'This is Anfield' on that plaque, Shankly explained: 'Son, players know that when they come to Liverpool, they face a hard task. Our side of the present day is a great side. But we remind visitors of our tradition as well. Our great side, plus the tradition of Liverpool Football Club, are an unbeatable combination.'

How right he was. It's enough to give any player a scary feeling when he realises that he has to play against Liverpool, their tradition and their Kop ... at Anfield. Tradition is a magical word that invites both awe and scorn; without doubt, when used in an alliance such as above, tradition is a very powerful weapon. We had arrived twenty minutes late at a ground where we knew we faced a hell of a match – to be greeted by a blast of cold spine-shivers from that plaque. 'Shanks' knew the value of tradition. But not everyone does when you enter football.

You are entering a profession – a world – where tradition and superstition reign supreme. It is important that you know how to cope with both, how to enjoy both and benefit from both. What is tradition? What are the origins of age-old superstitions? I believe it is worth examining the origins of two very important aspects of professional football and football clubs. In a nutshell: superstition comes first, tradition follows, then the tradition becomes something of a ritual superstition! This is not quite the double-Dutch it may appear.

We have talked about Bill Shankly – amazing how so many football stories involve 'Shanks' – and those burnt steaks. As a player with Preston, Shankly ate burnt steak before a match. Then, it was purely Shankly's own superstition. But he enjoyed it, looked upon it as a ritual, and carried it with him to Liverpool. As soon as Shankly began ordering burnt steaks for his players, the situation was no longer a superstition. It developed into a tradition.

Those Liverpool players – certainly some of them – will go on eating burnt steaks before a match. They will not question why. They will accept the steaks as part of their traditional pre-match meal. The crunch comes when, at some time, for whatever reason, burnt steaks are not available.

Now the players *will* notice. In an instant they will resent the fact that one of their traditions has been broken. Why? Because the tradition has completed the full circle, and is once again their superstition.

Is it getting any clearer? I hope so. Because the whole structure of British football is built on a foundation of tradition and superstition. And unless you understand how and why you will be repeatedly surprised at the things you see, hear and experience.

Whatever you see or hear in football will be the result of things seen and heard years and years ago. In other words, what *is* football, *is* because it has always been. Things happened decades ago – when the game was experiencing a difficult birth into the organised structure as we know it now – and because those things were even vaguely successful, operational or simple to grasp, they continued. They became traditions. Whether it happens to be club colours, club badges, mottoes, customs or style, they all stem from the past. To discover the basic framework of football as we know it today, we must go back many years, back beyond the turn of this century to see when the first bolt was fixed in the first girder at the very concrete foundations of football.

Without turning this chapter into a musty history lesson, I want to provide you with an insight into your profession before you are enveloped by traditions and superstitions you do not understand. Let's begin at the top. Arsenal, like all football clubs, have regular board meetings, which they hold in the boardroom at Highbury. The directors begin by having lunch. This lunch has never varied. Not one Arsenal director can tell you when they *did not* have tripe and onions for lunch before a board meeting!

'Why tripe and onions?' I asked chairman Denis Hill-Wood. He said: 'Well, we've always had tripe and onions,' departing with a puzzled expression on his face. So it is a tradition. Perhaps it began as a superstition, or because one member of the original Arsenal board loved the meal. Whatever the reason, nobody has bothered – or perhaps the word is 'dared' – to change the menu.

107

The more basic superstitions/traditions of football are the match-day rituals of footballers, managers and coaches. There are players who insist that nothing other than poached eggs on match-day will do them any good. Others are convinced that they must tie their left boot-lace before their right. Everyone knows about the ritual of being the last player to leave the dressing-room and therefore the last player to walk on to the pitch. To some players, this little weekly ritual is very important. Woe betide the new player who arrives at a club, to find that he shares this same superstition with another member.

Imagine the scene on match-day. The new player and the regular tail-ender eye each other across the changing-room after the other lads have gone out. Neither player knows that the other wants to be the last man. So they fiddle and fumble about, hoping for the other to leave. Taken to the daftest possible conclusion, the situation may arise one day where two players are trying to shove each other through the dressing-room door while a vital cup-tie is about to begin.

There are countless examples of managers clinging to bent coins, rabbits' paws, worn-out suits and all manner of 'lucky' aids. These are intelligent, logical, professional men. Yet they are not prepared to tempt fate. Or is that the real reason for always having their superstition at hand? If you think that these examples are a stretch on the imagination, then surely Don Revie must take the prize from the top shelf.

When Leeds United, with Revie their manager, were quickly establishing a reputation as 'Champion Runners-up' in all competitions, the Leeds camp was told of a curse on their Elland Road stadium. The curse was laid by an aggrieved gypsy many years ago – possibly because that gypsy had witnessed his caravan being towed off the Leeds pitch at 2.45 p.m. one Saturday!

Don Revie brought in a Leeds United-supporting gypsy to remove the curse. Picture the scene – if you can. The tense moment when the gypsy walked out on to the pitch as Revie and the players and groundstaff stood watching. Then the wailing and gesticulating as the curse was lifted – enough to send a chill down any normal spine. An exaggeration? Maybe superstition is built on exaggeration. Who knows?

There is no doubting the fact that superstitions are part and parcel of football life. But I wonder how much importance is attached to the 'lucky' aspects of maintaining superstitions. If you develop a superstition whereby you must be the first player to have both boots on, what happens the day you beat all existing records by getting both boots on before the other players have taken off their shoes – then go out and lose? Do you immediately give up your little ritual? No, you do not. Because the luck element is not the most important element. You carry on doing your 'boot-routine' because you are used to doing it. Because being the first to get your boots on gives you a little challenge every match-day. There is also the equally important aspect of this routine helping to take your mind off worrying about the match. So you can see that what most people describe as superstitions are really rituals that have become part of the footballer's match-day routine.

When players are staying away from home on a Friday night – spending the night in a hotel before playing a match in, say, Manchester, Liverpool or Bristol – they have equally set rituals. Usually, some players retire to bed after their evening meal, possibly to watch a few hours of television before going to sleep. Others prefer to sit around and play cards. But some of the players have got to go to the cinema. It's not a case of wanting to see a particular film. They *always* go to the cinema when staying overnight in a strange hotel, and they do not want to break their living habits. Once they have been to the cinema, they return to their hotel, climb into bed and go to sleep, relaxed and prepared for the game the next day.

Managers and coaches are equally prone to quirks and habits – some you could describe as superstitions, others purely tradition. One coach I will always remember gave us one particular exercise to do during every training session. We began by doing the usual warm-up exercises, and that was when his 'specials' took place. Came the day I asked him

109

why we did this exercise – not because I objected to doing it but because it was doing us no physical good whatsoever. The truth was, he did not know why he gave us that exercise – except for the fact that *he* had always done it as a player – possibly without knowing why – and came to the conclusion that there must have been a reason. So that's how a useless, meaningless exercise may achieve immortality!

Never forget what I have told you about asking questions. There will be similar instances in your career. Do not accept them in puzzled silence. Ask. There may be a perfectly good explanation. If so, your worries are over. If there is no explanation, try and establish whether or not the instance dates back to another era. In that coach's case, he had opted for doing what came naturally and easily to him, instead of questioning something he did not understand. Rather like the fairy tale of the King's New Clothes. In fact the merry old monarch was stark naked as he walked down the street. But because it was alleged that only people of high intelligence could see the magic robes he was wearing, none of his subjects dared admit that all they could see was not for publication.

There are two sides to tradition – the amusing, likeable and warming side, and the side that makes players sweat in their sleep the night before a big match. Some of the people you will meet in football are what I describe as 'tradition-orientated'.

Newcastle went down to play Leeds United at Elland Road at the time when the League introduced a new ruling concerning club strip. Colours were not allowed to clash under any circumstances, and our black and white stripes technically clashed with Leeds' all-white strip. We switched therefore to our new change strip of yellow. The players thought no more about it. But there was a very different reaction up in the directors' box. One of Newcastle's directors asked why we were not playing in black and white stripes. He was angry and puzzled. When the reasons were explained to him by another director, he snapped: 'I'm not standing for this. How dare the League break our traditions.'

Clashing colours meant nothing to that director. He could not come to terms with watching his beloved Newcastle 'Magpies' wearing 'foreign' yellow shirts.

The other side of tradition is the side which could affect you. The Liverpool example is typical of what I mean. Shankly knew exactly what he was doing when he erected that plaque. He was highlighting something that everyone who walked down that corridor already knew but did not want to discuss. They were certainly not prepared to have the frightening facts written up on the wall.

Once you come to terms with the awesome side of tradition, you will be able to draw from the emotions created by that special brand of anticipation. You will be able to experience the flutters in the pit of your stomach – and turn them to strength rather than raw nerves.

Most traditions are great for the behind-the-scenes side of football. They are great to have, great to recall and worth holding on to. You will see the traditions and superstitions of your club every time you take a stroll through the trophy-room. Old photographs, the crusty old ball used in the 1880 or whatever FA Cup Final, faded silverware dating back to the club's early days and so on. Sometimes it is possible to sniff the past just by spending a little time, alone, in front of trophy cabinets.

So far, nothing that I have mentioned about superstitions or traditions shows the dangerous and detrimental side – the side which holds football back, and which seriously hinders the development of the game. They are coming up next.

You must accept traditions for what they are, make your own judgements and accept whatever benefits they produce; but you must not become influenced or overawed by the past – whether the past was a period of greatness or a period of great players. Too many players live in the shadows of their predecessors. Too many fans live in the past and waste time making futile comparisons between the players of today and those of yesterday. They make no allowances for the fact that football has changed radically since their era.

111

Unfortunately, players, and indeed whole teams, can suffer a form of mental paralysis caused by the haunting echoes from the trophy room down the corridor. They are never allowed to forget the traditions they must follow or the greatness they must match.

Newcastle's immensely impressive unbeaten run of FA cup finals at Wembley prior to their final against Liverpool in 1974 was the chief source of pressure exerted on the squad in the month leading up to the big match. Press, TV, radio, friends and relatives lost no opportunities to remind us of our tradition.

Joe Harvey showed the other side – the positive side – of tradition before Newcastle's Anglo-Italian cup final against Fiorentina in Italy in 1973 when his pre-match team-talk hammered home one relevant point: 'In my years as player, captain, coach and manager of Newcastle, I've never lost a cup final. I like it that way.'

I met a wonderful old character not long ago – a man in his mid-eighties – who was once a musical hall comedian and song-and-dance man. George was his name, and I will always remember him for something he told me. We were discussing character, personality football, and the entertainment business in general. Jutting out his chin and jabbing me with a knobbly finger, George said: 'Young man, they can never take away your personality – they can only impersonate you!' I was still thinking that over many hours later – a gem of wisdom stemming from years of experience.

I am passing on that gem to you. Always remember it. No matter what traditions weigh heavily on your head and back when you go out to play for your club, hold your head up, stick out your chest and tell the world that you are going to outdo those traditions, never mind uphold them!

Find your own path in football. Not a path based on the traditions or superstitions of others. This is where your own individuality must emerge to the full. To a great degree, you must rely on yourself. Never ignore the advice and help of others, learn and question at the same time, but you will reach a stage when you have to make the final decision – which path to choose, remembering that your path leads all the way into your future, beyond football, beyond the traditions and superstitions that will surround you.

Once opportunity comes your way, grab it. Develop your own style, work at it and aim at being the best in the business. Naturally, people will always liken you to a Matthews, a Law, a Moore, a Banks or whichever member of the Football Hall of Fame they believe you to resemble. Don't resent comparison – but don't be blinded by it either. Ask yourself why someone tells you that you remind them of, say, Denis Law. The answer is simple. Because Denis Law created his own style – made his own way in football and stamped his personality and individuality on the game. Only when you have done the same will future generations use your name when making similar comparisons.

A fan once came up to me and said: 'I've watched you play a number of times. Sometimes you remind me of "Dixie" Dean. On other occasions you show me a flash of the best of Jimmy Greaves.' I cut him off there. He had said enough. I did not intend to be rude. But I was making my own way in football. I did not want to be seen as a carbon copy – and therefore a poorer version – of a former 'great'.

Afterwards, however, when I was alone, I realised that it was not a bad thing to be told that parts of my game reminded that chap of such great players. There is certainly no harm in developing strengths and assets similar to those evident in great players. But that is a very different thing from deliberately setting out to become another so-and-so. But it was also important to that fan to have his memories re-lived, making them a stronger part of his life. Remember, that fan's life did not just begin five seconds before he met me: he has a past, and it is very important to him.

Mozart gave music lessons to keep body and soul together. His music was the toast of Europe. Yet, as was the case with so many men of genius, Mozart had to graft when he'd finished a day's composing, in order to eat that evening. One

113

of his early pupils was a serious-looking young German lad with very abrupt mannerisms, and little idea of politeness – in fact a character in total contrast to that of his tutor. Needing the money, Mozart ignored the social graces, or the lack of them, and gave the youngster piano lessons. Mozart was quick to spot a bit of talent there. He knew that he had a more than willing pupil. Yet neither pupil nor tutor realised the significance of what proved a brief interlude. Neither man nor boy could know how many millions of words, emotions and tears would result from those few music lessons.

Mozart died in his early thirties – basically of a combination of ailments that culminated in one illness too strong for his constitution. A pauper's grave – unmarked into the bargain – was his resting place. Meanwhile his former pupil was turning out musical masterpieces by the dozen. A great pity that Wolfgang Mozart never really got to know Ludwig Beethoven!

I offer Mozart and Beethoven as a classical example (couldn't resist that one) because who would dare to say that Beethoven was 'another Mozart' – yet who can deny that Beethoven's development of the symphonic work was influenced by Mozart's early teaching and by Mozart's own compositions – listened to with respect and dedication by the young Beethoven. The young pupil chose his own path and made his own way in his particular field. He emulated nobody. But he certainly benefited by learning from another great of the same field.

You must decide from the outset that you are going to be somebody special – yourself. Only impersonators will get anywhere near to re-creating the original you. It is sad when a young player reveals to everyone the fact that he has not chosen his own path and that he is genuinely influenced and affected by the superstitions and traditions within football.

One young player once approached me in the changing-room before a game and said: 'Why do you always smear Vaseline over your eyebrows?' I looked at him for a few seconds to see if my leg was being pulled, but his face was serious and very straight. 'I beg your pardon?' I said. 'Well, I'm puzzled by the Vaseline,' he continued. 'It's like a ritual with you. You smear it across your eyebrows before every match. And you told me that you don't believe in superstitions.' I replied: 'Yes, that's correct. I don't believe in superstitions. But if you would like to think of this as my one superstition, do so by all means. But let me tell you it's a superstition that does not allow sweat to flow into my eyes!' He's still looking at me now.

TEN

Wembley –
the Magic and the Misery

Every time I walk through the front door of my home, I am reminded of Wembley. Why? Because the loser's medal from the 1974 FA Cup Final and the loser's tankard from the 1976 Football League Cup Final are positioned where I have to look at them every day. Those two momentoes serve as a constant reminder of how it feels to be a loser. And every time I see them, I reaffirm my vow never again to be a Wembley 'runner-up'.

I never thought that losing a second Wembley Cup Final could be as painful an experience as losing your first Cup Final. But it is much, much worse. Any player who has played at Wembley and lost, consoles himself with the personal promise that he will be back, and that next time he will be a winner. So imagine the agony of appearing in two Wembley Finals and losing both. This agony becomes magnified when you realise that the majority of professional footballers never have the opportunity of playing at Wembley, and a minority cherish their one unforgettable appearance for the rest of their lives.

In 1974, I was a member of a Newcastle team destined to give one of the poorest Cup Final performances of all time. We never got going and Liverpool fully deserved their resounding 3-0 victory. Two years later, however, Newcastle and Manchester City provided 100,000 Wembley fans with an exciting League Cup Final. Unfortunately, City pipped us 2-1, and while we were glad to have shown ourselves in a better light after the 1974 fiasco, nothing could take away the awful disappointment that comes with defeat.

You may play at Wembley at some stage in your career. You may appear in one of the two major domestic Cup Finals, the Charity Shield match or even for your country.

I have tasted Wembley's wine and vinegar, experienced the magic and the misery of playing at England's football Mecca, walked off the hallowed turf in ecstasy and despair. I want you to be prepared for Wembley. I want you to be able to grab your big opportunity, if it comes your way, and be armed with sufficient knowledge and background information to overcome the incredible pressures that accompany any big match at Wembley. Believe me, there is a lot more to playing at Wembley than giving a handful of interviews, looking smart for the day and shaking hands with royalty.

There are certain occasions, certain big events in all walks of life, that can affect people in a way that nothing else can affect them. To the professional footballer, playing at Wembley is one of those occasions. Make no mistake, Wembley casts its spell no matter how many times you play there. But at least your second visit, while just as gut-wrenching as the first, does not come as a complete shock and surprise to the system. Had I always known failure at Wembley, I doubt if I would have been able to discuss this subject. But with the misery of two Cup Final defeats, I also have two very happy memories.

I returned to Wembley nine months or so after the FA Cup Final, still shuddering at the memory of watching Liverpool going up the steps to collect that beautiful silver pot. This time, however, I was wearing the white shirt of England, and I was determined to end what had proved a scoring duck for my country since I had won my first cap against Wales in 1972. Our opponents? World Champions West Germany, unbeaten since their World Cup Final victory over Holland in 1974 and led by that brilliant football artist, Franz Beckenbauer.

What a night that was! We murdered them. Alan Ball covered every inch of the park, the England defence snuffed out Germany's stuttering attacks, and a skilful young man named Alan Hudson swaggered through midfield with all the arrogance shown by Germany's Gunther Netzer at Wembley in 1972 when they won 3-1. Colin Bell fired England ahead, and when 'Bally' flighted a right-wing cross to the far post, I headed past Sepp Maier to make it 2-0 and break that duck.

But my lasting memory of that night was seeing Beckenbauer stumble as he challenged me and finish up on his bum on the edge of his own area. If only I could have raced up those steps to collect that beautiful silver pot that night ... but winning for England was magical enough on its own.

Sometimes, the players in your team can make or break your Wembley day. In 1974, none of the Newcastle players could get going. We were unable to help each other. But one month after beating West Germany, I was back at Wembley as England faced Cyprus in a European Championship tie.

That night, I appreciated what it can mean to have a great player playing alongside you: Alan Ball kept on at me, before and during the match, about how many goals I should score. When I got the first, he came up and said: 'That's just the first.' When I had reached four, 'Bally' kept reminding me of the individual international scoring record and he never let up until I'd scored number five and equalled that record.

Players such as Alan Ball have the ability to motivate the players around them. He helped me more that night than anyone watching the match ever knew. So we won 5-0 and I went home clutching the match-ball. That ball is also placed where I can see it every time I walk through the door. Oddly enough, my eyes usually fasten on to those two loser's medals!

Yes, I have experienced the magic and the misery of Wembley. But now it is time for you to experience the whole situation from the beginning – to go through the 'Wembley Mincer', from the moment you walk off the field after winning a major Cup semi-final, and the massive publicity machine grinds into motion.

Without doubt, you must have watched countless Cup Finals, either on television or from the Wembley terraces.

You have absorbed the atmosphere, thrilled to the singing and the massive waves of emotion that sweep around the oval-shaped stadium. You have day-dreamed about playing at Wembley, spent many nights lying awake just thinking about the Cup Final, especially if the team you follow happens to be playing. But like so many lads of your age and with your dreams, you have no idea of what playing at Wembley entails, what it can do to a perfectly sane, rational young man and what lasting scars it can leave.

I have seen good players freeze at Wembley, go to pieces and literally long to get off the pitch and away from the thousands of eyes that focus on every tiny mistake. I have also seen players reach incredible heights, even to the point where they have surpassed all previous form, because they have been inspired by the whole occasion. So much depends on the reaction of the individual as he walks out of the players' tunnel and hears the frightening roar of the 100,000 fans for the first time. Very often, this is the moment of truth – this is where Cup Final teams are made or broken. And you can tell by glancing at the players beside you.

But already I have whisked you into Wembley when there is so much to experience before you ever see the peg in the dressing-room. My first warning should be heeded the moment you realise that you have reached Wembley.

Wembley Stadium is the palace of English football. It is the one ground, above all club grounds, where people expect to see the best there is of English football. But this is not always the case. The reasons for this have already been given. The vastness of the stadium, the volume of noise, the complete circle of faces that contort and distort in joy and fervour: all serve to either inspire or terrify. Too often, it is the latter. Games billed as 'certain classics' have turned out to be a total anti-climax. Some have bordered on the absolute yawn.

Yet reaching a Cup Final is the most exciting experience any player can have, certainly at a domestic level. Players look forward to Wembley with such intensity that by match-day they are as wound-up as springs. No player goes out with the deliberate intention of ruining the show-piece

119

day of the season. But circumstances can wreck his well-laid plans, his dreams and his countless vows, made to family, friends, colleagues and the media.

So the week of planning is over. The manager has called his final get-together. The players are longing to begin the trip to Wembley. Because suddenly, the tension is getting to them, despite all attempts to remain calm and relaxed. The level of nervous chatter, badly-played card-hands and woeful jokes increases as the team coach arrives in the first road from which the twin towers can be clearly seen. Then comes the long, slow crawl through the milling fans down Olympic Way. The stadium is always looming large ahead, so near yet miles away because you cannot jump off the coach and dive through the players' entrance. By now, the butterflies in your stomach have become bats and nerves are so stretched that a decent musician could probably play a quick tune on the team's back-four.

Outside the coach, your fans are waving their flags, banners and scarves, cheering and encouraging. Your opponents' followers quickly spot 'the enemy' and waste no time in letting you know what they think of your chances. Fans are always extrovert, loud and determined to make their point. Players become accustomed to cheers and jeers. Yet on the crawl up to the stadium, those fans seem larger, louder, more demanding and more frightening. They are all part of the day – all associated with the occasion which by now is tearing your stomach apart.

For the 'first-timer' on the coach – those players who have never played at Wembley before – their feelings could be likened to those of the raw recruit who is told that his next stint of duty is in the front line, right up at the front, facing the unknown. And when you consider that in many cases the first-timers heavily outnumber the 'I've seen it all before' characters, you can imagine the atmosphere on that team-coach. Not that the lads who have played at Wembley before are any less nervous. It is just that they are not so shattered by the nerves. They know what to expect, but still feel watery around the knee-joints.

Knowing that you are going to be nervous in no way helps to calm you down – as I discovered. Because the gradual build-up of publicity through the time between winning the semi-final and going to Wembley is so powerful that even the most seasoned professional feels the wobbles when he is suddenly confronted with the hour-by-hour countdown to the kick-off.

If it were possible to take a cold, hard, unfeeling look at the whole situation, the pumping adrenalin and the churning stomachs would be difficult to understand. All the same, the players are only being asked to go out, well supported, and play a game of football – something they have done time and time again.

But not at Wembley. The very name brings a tingle to the spines of most footballers. You will be no different when your time comes. So do not be either worried or surprised. Only start to question your emotions if the whole business leaves you cold and unaffected. Then, I would say, there is something missing from your make-up as a professional footballer.

The crunch of such a cold analysis would come when the root-cause of the nerves was found. Unlike any other game of football, this one game at Wembley cannot be lost. The thought of losing is enough to make players light-headed and sweaty. No player likes losing. But in some games defeat, while never acceptable, is sometimes bearable and understandable because of various circumstances. But not a Wembley Cup Final. Because it may be the one and only chance a player gets in his entire career. Ironically, the very pressure caused by the occasion proves too much for many players. They may have been Cup heroes *en route* to the Final, brilliant in every round. But such statistics mean nothing when the big day arrives. Countless dreams have been smashed beyond repair in ninety minutes under the twin towers.

Yet the thought of playing a major Cup Final anywhere other than Wembley immediately detracts from the whole charisma of the occasion. The fuss that followed the disappointing League Cup Final between Aston Villa and Everton

121

last season is a good example of what I mean. That Final was a bore, a flop, a 0–0 draw. But there was no extra time, and the point most people made when they heard that the replay was to be at Sheffield Wednesday's Hillsbrough Ground was: 'Who cares about a League Cup Final played in Sheffield on a freezing night?' Who cares indeed. Take away Wembley, and the competition itself loses much of its value and its attraction. But I do agree with people who say that England should play their international matches on grounds such as Old Trafford, Anfield, Goodison Park and Villa Park. The crowd are that much closer to the action, the atmosphere is more familiar to Football League players and the whole set-up is less appealing to the visiting nation.

Wembley – certainly at international level – is too much of a leveller. Some England players freeze and struggle, often failing to find their excellent club form, while visiting teams relish their first game at Wembley, rise to the occasion and play above their usual capabilities. Hardly a bagful of advantages to the England team!

All thoughts on Wembley suddenly vanish as the coach pulls up outside the players' entrance. Whatever has been running through their minds is interrupted. Now they can get off the coach and stretch their legs, flex their nerves. The mounted police keep the crowd at bay as the players file off, trying to show a brave, uncaring face, smiling and winking while all the time longing to embrace the seclusion of the door ahead.

Now, perhaps, is the time when some of the players think back on what they said to that grinning character who bounded on to the team-coach with a microphone and thrust it under their noses. Half-way down Olympic Way, he appeared with a list of searching questions such as: 'Well, do you think you will win?' Resisting the temptation to reply: 'No, I'm only here to mend the plumbing,' you tend to dive straight in, only too glad of the distraction. It is so nice to have something to take your mind off the nerves. Perhaps some of the answers are a little far-fetched, but who cares? The fans love it, the media love it and the players are grateful for the opportunity to waffle away their anxious moments.

The first thing that strikes the players when they enter the stadium is the antiquated, cathedral-like, forbidding appearance of the place of which they have dreamt for so many years. But fortunately there is little time to brood on it – because now it's straight to the dressing-room. Once you get changed, everything is done strictly according to a detailed programme, because this is not your ordinary game where you can run out and have a relaxing kick-about as soon as you are all ready. The steward raps on your dressing-room door, and demands that you be ready in two minutes. Here is another mental shocker. Where you normally trot out two minutes or so before the kick-off, here you are rushed out into the corridor where you must wait, and wait and wait.

You have done your warm-up, your stretches, your legs are oiled. The nervous chatter grows louder. Some lads jog on the spot, others fumble around for a piece of chewing-gum. Away above you, the sound of the band and the chanting thousands filters down. But you see nothing. You are lined up in two single files with the managers up front and the referee and his linesmen in front of them.

Then, at last, you get the word: 'Let's go.' It is a long walk up that tunnel, and the noise of the crowd gets louder and louder. Then, all of a sudden, with a few yards to go, the smell of stale beer and hot-dogs hits you square in the face – as if you weren't queasy enough already.

When you step out of that tunnel, the noise is enough to knock you off your feet. Perhaps you have stood in a Wembley crowd and been part of the roar. Perhaps you have sat up in the seats and enjoyed the atmosphere. But you have no idea how loud is that roar until you hear it while emerging from the mouth of that tunnel.

As I said earlier, this is the moment when the legs turn to jelly, when the spine-tingles feel like pin-pricks. As the full blast of the atmosphere hits you, your day is either made or smashed. Even if you feel up to it, there is the fleeting desire to turn on your new studs and race back down the tunnel. I

123

don't think any player has actually made that dash, but I know many have thrown a quick glance longingly over their shoulder.

The two columns march across the pitch until they are standing, facing one another, under the Royal Box. The players are keyed up and longing to go. They have done their warm-up routines but they begin to feel cold. And now they have to endure the presentation ceremony.

Slowly, the party comprising the officials and the attending member of the Royal Family make their way along the line of players. It is very embarrassing, if you have just been smearing Vaseline across your eyebrows and oil on your legs, to have to shake hands with royalty. Between greasy hands and the powerful smell of liniment, the pre-Cup Final player must be something out of the ordinary for the royal guest. The emotional drain speeds up as the national anthem is played and the players would probably give anything to just curl up in a bed and go to sleep.

Finally, after one-and-a-half lifetimes, the game starts – and it is almost an anti-climax! After all the rigmarole beforehand, the actual job of playing comes easily and as something of a relief. But the overwhelming feeling is not one of 'remember that this is the big occasion and must be an entertaining spectacle.' No, the players are aware only of all the hard work and graft they have put in on their way to the Final.

You will experience the very same feelings: I must win at all costs; I can't throw everything away, everything that I have worked for and dreamed of all season, in ninety minutes – and this is where the Wembley pitch gets blamed for just about everything bar World War II.

People say the pitch is tiring and draining. But I don't agree. It is a big pitch, but it is better than most of the League ground pitches the players play on throughout the seasons. No, what will bring on your cramp and force you to roll down your socks is the occasion, not the pitch. You will run harder than at any other time in the season. You will burn off more nervous energy than ever before. You will test your physical capabilities to the limits without even knowing you are doing so. The desire to win will drive you on until suddenly, cramp will send that searing pain through your leg. But don't accuse the Wembley pitch of spoiling your day. This is one of the myths that has been allowed to grow out of all proportion.

If you lose, you walk off the pitch absolutely shattered. You have spent every last drop of energy in your body only to come second, to be second up those steps. You know that thousands of your supporters are heartbroken with you. European football will not be yours next season. Exhaustion and disappointment take their toll. For victory, please read all the opposites! Nothing will prevent you from doing a lap of honour. Cramp disappears, so does any feeling of general tiredness. You will bound up those steps.

People say that it is better to have played at Wembley and lost than never to have played there at all. I say it over and over, but I am not sure. Wembley has some happy memories for me, but mainly the memories are sad ones because they are of losing. And nobody wants to know about or hear about losing or losers.

If you get your Wembley chance, be a winner. Remember what I have told you, remember what lies in store for you. Do not be overawed by what happens before the Final. Expect it, handle it, be master of it. Nothing will stem the nervous flood that is sure to sweep you up Olympic Way. But at least be aware of why it is happening and what you must do to get everything into perspective – *win!*

ELEVEN
Referees

David Price could not have picked a better match in which to score his first League goal. Arsenal had lost their previous seven First Division matches – the worst League run in the club's history – so our match at Stoke was vitally important.

Another defeat would have cast the players into a depression born of frustration, worry and draining confidence. We had to get a result. But then so did Stoke. Relegation threatened, and the resignation two days previously of manager Tony Waddington made the match important to both clubs.

When David Price rose to head his all-important goal after just over one minute, our spirits rose with him. Even when Terry Conroy curled a beauty over Jimmy Rimmer to equalise a few minutes later, we were into our stride and beginning to play a bit.

Then came the moment of disaster. Liam 'Chippy' Brady was sent off. What angered the Arsenal players was that they had seen it coming for some minutes, but could do nothing about it. Only the referee could have prevented the incident – and he, as is often the case with referees, saw what was happening but was unable to interpret what he saw.

I believe that the only way to solve what is a massive problem in football is to appoint professional referees. There is no other way of bringing referees and players closer together. It is more than a case of simply paying them more money – they must have a greater understanding of players and of the intricacies of the modern game.

'Chippy' Brady, always a dangerous player on the ball, was in the kind of form defenders dread. So when Steve Waddington, son of former manager Tony, fouled him, nobody was very surprised. Minutes later, 'Chippy' was again brought down by Waddington. Again, referee Trelford Mills did nothing about the offender, deeming it more important that the ball, which had rolled off for a goal-kick, be placed on the exact, correct spot! When the third foul occurred, in the twenty-fourth minute, 'Chippy' lost his temper and shoved his arm in Waddington's face. Referee Mills came over, booked Waddington and sent off 'Chippy' for retaliation. 'Chippy' knew that he had done wrong. He appreciated that his loss of temper had left us to battle for sixty-six minutes with ten men – away from home. Yet, without defending his act of retaliation, I question the whole system where the amateur official holds the professional's career in his hands. Where was the protection for 'Chippy'? Have no doubts, had the incident not erupted into a sending-off affair, Waddington would not have been booked – despite committing three fouls, within minutes, on the same opponent.

My advice to you in such a situation is again very simple. Never retaliate. Get up and walk away, if possible. Nothing upsets a clogger more than an opponent who takes all the stick without losing his head. It may seem a lot easier to say than to do, but one's mind must be conditioned to acceptance of 'stick' and to overcome the immediate reaction of physical retaliation. This will then lead to a cool, calculating head at all times, especially when under pressure of any kind, in any walk of life.

I have taken stick from all kinds of players. Some can give and take, physically, in a hard-fought game – players such as Gordon McQueen of Leeds United. Others want to knock lumps off you, but go to pieces if you give them a tough time.

Some people reading this section of the chapter will

immediately understand what I am talking about; others will not understand fully, because I am talking the language of football, the language of the professional – a language few referees ever learn. This is where and why the refereeing system breaks down.

The referee at Stoke saw Waddington foul Brady. But he did not see beyond the situation. Nor did he appreciate the importance of swift and fair action. A smouldering situation could so easily have been defused in seconds – had Mr Mills fully understood what was going on. The match was probably ruined as a spectacle for the crowd, and was certainly ruined for both teams. Arsenal were left with no alternative but to close ranks more than we had planned, and Stoke were left to try to prise our tighter defence apart. I am sure they would have preferred to play against eleven men in a match that would have been a more even, properly balanced contest. So would we.

You will meet the same situation 'Chippy' Brady experienced. What worries me is – will the match official see the situation developing in time to prevent it from boiling over? Not if he is an amateur referee. Equally, you will sometimes find yourself in Waddington's over-enthusiastic boots. But again, will the referee be sharp enough to pull you up, calm you down and prevent your enthusiasm from getting out of hand? Not if he is an amateur.

The whole problem stems from the fact that referees are not professionals. They do not spend their whole week in football, working with players, getting to know players as men as well as professional footballers. Referees do not understand or speak the language of the game. They understand the laws as set out in the text-book (although they rarely agree on their interpretations of those laws), but they have no way of getting underneath the skins of the men to whom they apply those laws.

The pro player earns his bread and butter by playing. The amateur referee earns a bit of pocket money and has a good time. The respective worlds of professional player and referee are seen to be galaxies apart once a match ends. The referee has a shower or bath, relaxes with a drink and goes home. On Sunday he takes his family out for a walk or a drive. On Monday he returns to his office desk or factory floor. The player, however, may spend most of his weekend lying on the treatment table, having an injury treated by the club physiotherapist or doctor.

The frightening fact is that the professional footballer's injury may have been sustained as a direct result of the amateur referee's lack of understanding, lack of comprehension of what really went on during the ninety minutes he refereed. Every Saturday, players have to absorb punishment that no human being should have to experience. Their whole career can be wrecked, ended, shattered by one battering too many. I am afraid that no amount of 'tightening up on the laws' will improve, or ever can improve matters. We must, for the sake of every young player who is prepared to lay his future on the line, introduce and perfect a system whereby referees are able to spend their whole week working, training and virtually living with their local professional club. Only then will referees 'get into' professional football sufficiently to understand all that they see during a match, and the people they are handling. They must talk with professionals every day, join in their chats, their rows, their traumas and their laughter. There is no other way of learning about the men, and the game, they control.

I have met some great referees. Clive Thomas is one. There was a time when Clive Thomas earned the reputation of 'Clive the Book' because of his conviction that booking players was the only way to solve problems on the field. Those days are long past. Clive Thomas is now one of the best referees in Europe. Why? Because he has taken the trouble to learn about the men he referees. He knows the tricks of the trade and understands the pressures that build up during a game. Thomas has worked hard to get on the professional wavelength. As a result, he commands respect - from professional footballers and the public alike. He is without doubt the most professional of our amateur referees.

Men such as Clive Thomas are better equipped to look after players such as you. A youngster, playing in his first few League games, needs a bit of a shoulder to lean upon from his team-mates. But he also needs the watchful eye of an experienced, knowledgable referee who will spot situations involving the young player almost before those situations develop.

The experienced, professional referee will see the hardened old pro shaping up to let you know who is boss. The referee will know what happens in a crowded goalmouth when you go up in a wedge of bodies to challenge for the ball. The referee will have his eyes firmly on the old pro with the angled elbows. The moment he is pulled up, the old pro realises that he has been spotted. He accepts the fact that the referee is his match, and backs off. This sharp refereeing also prevents the inevitable situation where your team-mates go looking for the old pro to wage their vendetta on him because of his treatment of you. Oh yes, there are many sides to that old coin.

These situations build up in a match, often without the fans realising what is going on before their eyes. They follow the movements of the ball. So, too, do most amateur officials. They are more worried about missing seeing the ball edge out of play for a split second than they are about keeping an eye on the off-the-ball incidents that provoke and prelude so many ugly scenes.

Preventive medicine is the best. The professional referee, having probably seen all the tricks in action during club training games, will not be hoodwinked. His whistle will beat the crunching tackle or the jabbing elbow every time. The amateur is left with his notebook crammed with names, the howling derision of thousands of irritated, frustrated spectators in his ears, and the knowledge that no matter how many red or yellow cards he waves, he has lost control of the match.

You will have heard, time and again, that the standard of football in Britain trails behind standards abroad. Perhaps this problem will be solved by the time you enter the game. There are defects in our football and in our system of coaching and developing young players. By now, you know all my feelings concerning this subject! Let's just say that the repairs to be done on our national game will take time.

We do, however, have a wonderful opportunity to set an example to the rest of Europe – an example they would have to follow. We can become the pathfinders in the field of professional refereeing. We already have the best referees in the world, but this is not enough.

Let us examine the advantages. We have established that the professional referee would be able to spend more time in the game as opposed to training, as often as possible, on his own, after a hard day's work at the office. But I am not claiming that by paying our referees we would automatically improve the standard of refereeing. What I am saying is that if referees had the financial security of a profession, they could spend more time in football, become part and parcel of the game rather than continue as 'the loneliest men in football' – in other words 'outsiders'.

When you become a professional footballer, you gamble your whole future on whether or not you can become one of the small minority in football who are successful enough to provide sufficiently for their post-playing career, or are fortunate enough to obtain a position at coaching or managerial level. If you fail to achieve this level of security, you join the majority of players, who in their early or mid-thirties hope to find employment after their careers in football finish. You may perhaps, want to be a salesman or take a brewery course in the hope of eventually becoming a publican. With a large slice of luck, you may possibly be able to purchase a small corner shop with your meagre savings – and with the help of a bank loan. This is the lot of the footballer who fails to make the top grades.

So am I being fair to referees to suggest a system that will leave them jobless during their early fifties? I believe I am.

131

The Referees' Association can easily acquaint their members with pension schemes and the rest. But what I see as being of fundamental importance is that both referees and players will be in the same situation – giving greater all-round understanding and showing foresight of situations and predicaments both on and off the field of play. As professionals, both players and referees must look to their futures from the same standpoint.

I have mentioned before some of the educational courses available to footballers during their careers. The Football League, the Referees' Association and the Professional Footballers' Association, working in conjunction, could bring about the 'Course of Professional Refereeing'. A footballer who retires in his early thirties knowing that he cannot continue to achieve proper match-fitness throughout the physically demanding football season would most certainly be fit enough to referee at top level. I hear a referee telling me that an educational course is all very well, but not enough in itself without a great deal of practical work as well, and I agree. But the course must provide the practical work as well as teach the laws of the game, positional knowledge and all the workings of the job.

For example, a Third Division player, having just graduated from the classroom, can move on to referee Sunday football and steadily progress up to levels such as the Athenian, Isthmian and London-Spartan Leagues, then the semi-professional Northern Premier and Southern Leagues. Naturally, he will have to confine his refereeing work to mid-week matches once he graduates beyond Sunday morning football. Don't forget, this player is still playing for a Third Division club who may even demand that a percentage of his midweek games be sacrificed. But no matter how many games he referees during his playing career, those games will prove invaluable experience once he begins to think in terms of the Football League list.

I imagine there would be fifty professional referees, or thereabouts, in three grades. The first grade would comprise the élite: about five referees who would generally handle the crucial matches on the programme – the matches crying out for experience and top-class refereeing. UEFA would have their pick of these men for their top European ties and for international matches.

I am tired of hearing about referees 'having the honour' of handling the FA Cup or Football League Cup Finals. What makes me really sick is the fact that the job usually goes to a referee who has been around for some time, and who, in the eyes of the powers that be, deserves to have this 'honour'. There is no honour of occasion whilst the job is being done, only afterwards, when the job has been *successfully* done; when the referee has been to Wembley, refereed and had a very good game. Such games should be handled by the man who, at the time, is deemed to be the man in form – the best referee. Teams do not select players for such games out of sentiment. Why should referees be there for any other reason than the fact that they are 'the' referee of the season?

By now I expect you are nodding off in the corner. But I want you to understand that there is another avenue for you to explore when your career comes to an end. I have only just scratched the surface of the refereeing subject. It merits a book. But having said that, there are no laws or systems so perfect that they cannot be changed.

What about the referees you will encounter? There are as many different characters on the Football League list of referees as there are in any League club squad. Everybody· in football knows the high-stepping style of Derek Nippard, the 'Pickwickian' whiskers and extrovert mannerisms of Roger Kirkpatrick, the stern expression and towering frame of Jack Taylor. No doubt there will be referees whom you will like and those to whom you will take a dislike. It works the same both ways. Refs, too, have their likes and dislikes. This is often a chemical thing, human nature – call it what you like, it happens. Be prepared.

I dislike extrovert officials who go out of their way to make

133

their mark on a game. The best referees I have met are the men who have a quiet but firm word in your ear as they run by. No posing, no waving finger and yawning mouth for the benefit of the TV cameras or the Sunday newspaper photographers. The good referees are the men who rarely become involved in dissent situations: a player who steps out of line and is caught, knows he has done wrong and can accept his medicine if it is properly and professionally administered. There is nothing more potentially explosive than the situation where the referee stops the match, to the disgust of the fans who have paid to see action, and proceeds to lecture a player as if he were addressing a naughty schoolboy. The player immediately feels contempt towards the referee. Even if he is completely in the wrong, and knows it, the player allows his emotions to rule. They are already stretched by the tension of the match. Being made to look a fool in front of thousands of fans is often the last straw.

Referees are not always right. They know it. Players know it. Clive Thomas wins my respect because he is man enough to admit when he has made a mistake. Too many referees are not. I remember trotting past Thomas during a match and saying: 'Bad decision there, ref.' He turned to me and replied: 'Yes, I know. But haven't you made a few mistakes today?' Yes, I had. And I did not enjoy being reminded of them. I had to admire the man. I still do.

Jack Taylor put the whole job of refereeing into perspective when he said: 'The referee is the stage-manager. He does not have a part in the production – not even the part of the wicked uncle. Not so much as a walk-on part. He is the figure in the background. His job is to ensure that all twenty-two players are allowed to play their game.' I go along with that sentiment all the way. I will not hammer a referee who makes a blunder, even if it is to my disadvantage. But I will hammer the man who attempts to grab the spotlight at the expense of professional football as the spectacle.

You must make your own decisions in life. Some of those

134

decisions may be directly affected by decisions made by another man – the referee. Just hope that by the time you are a professional, the referee who handles your first match is also a professional.

TWELVE
A Week in the Life

Footballers are creatures of habit. You will not be an exception to that rule. There is a good and valid reason why footballers enjoy a routine existence. They live and work in a world, a profession that is basically insecure. A routine provides a certain kind of security.

When you begin to worry about your form, or when a nagging injury refuses to heal and you are missing matches, you will appreciate the weekly routine because it serves to remind you that you still belong, that you still have a niche in the club. Without being fully conscious of the fact, you will value your routine as the foundation stone of your career. Without it, you would immediately feel lost and disorientated. Most footballers are totally unaware of their reliance on their routine until someone or something forces them to interrupt their regular schedule. Then they experience the disturbing sense of being dragged off course.

The question often asked is, does a routine life produce positive or negative results? Overall, I would say 'positive'. The actual job of playing football is often skimmed over by those who write about the game, and often overlooked by many who work within it. What is so often disregarded is the extremely important 'habit factor'. Playing football entails fitness, ability, dedication and often nerve. But there is another ingredient, one which rarely gets a mention, perhaps because it lacks the immediate impact of the other four good habits.

When you analyse the game of football, a lot of very

136

exciting and entertaining incidents, moves and moments are not simply the result of instinctive genius on the part of one player. Sometimes, genius is the producer. But in a lot of cases the practising of good habits is behind good results. The professional footballer who develops good habits through his routine life within the game is generally the footballer who makes few bad errors.

Mind you, it is said – and I do not deny the fact – that my one real habit is that I like to lie in bed for as long as possible on the morning of a match-day.

It is important that you appreciate from the beginning that your life as a professional footballer will entail routine. People often make the mistake of assuming that only civil servants and office workers are either blessed or cursed – whichever way you view it – with routine lives.

Your life as a professional footballer will revolve around your club and your team-mates. You will make countless social plans only to see them dashed. You will have long-standing appointments and dinner-dates overruled by unexpected midweek matches.

Injury of any kind will either keep you in bed or add to your routine schedule between home and club and home again. Lose the lingering idea, once and for all, that the footballer is footloose and fancy-free. Far from it, very far from it – unless he wants to drift on to the soccer scrapheap. If you want to join the sad percentage of young players who decide to go their own way, you will not establish any precedents, nor will you become football's rebel with or without a cause. You will just become a football bum.

Don't be frightened by the realisation that you are caught up in a weekly routine. Accept the fact, value the reality of it all. Don't set out to knock your way of life just for the sake of making noise.

What you must do is question every day of your life – not to be troublesome or destructive, but just to ensure that you always know and understand why you are doing what you are doing. Routine is one thing. Allowing yourself to drift along like an unthinking, programmed zombie is another. Always be aware of what you are doing.

At the end of the day you must get your young life into perspective, quickly. Only then will your professional routine become acceptable, and the many interruptions to that routine become tolerable.

For the sake of making the point, and hammering it home, I will take you through a typical week in my life. As you will see, most of my well-laid plans to beat the sameness of any one day end up in the bin. And, ironically, I am usually happy that they do.

Training schedules are only altered to suit fixtures. Basically, there are two programmes: training during a week with a midweek match, and training during a week without a midweek match. Not that you work any more or less. It is just a matter of juggling schedules around a little to make sure nothing is overdone, underdone or completely missed.

The week I have chosen is one where we did not play a midweek match. Most weeks of a season follow that pattern, and I want you to see what can happen and does happen to a professional footballer during any normal family week. Some day, you will go through many such weeks. Some will bring unexpected bonuses, either at home or at the club. Other weeks will provide you with stiff tests of character. You must learn to take everything in your stride, the praise, the insults, the invasions of privacy, the day-to-day happenings at your club.

Sunday The noise filters through from the kitchen, along the corridor and up to the rim of my pillow. My eyelids battle against all natural instincts, and open. It has to be Sunday.

When you have three daughters – and a two-month-old golden labrador pup – it is easy to tell what day it is. Monday mornings are always quiet, almost sullen, because it is time to go back to school. But Sundays – that's a very different proposition.

The rumble becomes thunder as footsteps approach the door. Attempts to hide under the bedclothes are futile. If the girls don't get me, Jasper's cold wet nose rockets up from the foot of the bed like a torpedo. It's time to get up. I wave a corner of white sheet in the air as a signal of surrender.

Now for the battle to the bathroom. Having negotiated toys, dolls and almost broken my neck on Jasper's rubber bone (I must take that damn tinkling bell out of it) I shut the door and relive yesterday's 2-1 win at Coventry as the water washes away the stiffness and sleepiness. I scored a first-minute goal and we took it from there.

Lots to think about, but first I have to make breakfast. I always make the breakfast on Sundays. Julie enjoys her lie-in and never complains about burnt toast or watery coffee.

When we win I always make a point of flicking through the Sunday papers. But when we lose, I usually miss that 'treat' and concentrate on enjoying my day with my family.

Jasper is making 'walkies' noises, and with a new carpet just laid, I'm taking no chances. Off we go – on a bitterly cold morning – for a trundle up the country lane. My mind still flashing back to incidents from the match at Coventry while Jasper jerks me to a standstill every few yards to investigate a rustle in the bushes or an inviting tree.

By the time I get home, my daughters – Claire, Jeanette and Louise – are standing in a very pointed huddle, wrapped up to their ears in coats, scarves and mittens. Just enough time for a hot coffee before I head out into the winter air for another 'healthy' trudge.

To be truthful, I love it. My daughters read me like a book. Kids can slaughter you with one cutting, totally honest observation. Jeanette, by now covered in mud, says: 'Come on daddy, we're muddy and if you're muddy too, mummy will have to be angry with all of us.' So I get muddy. Who cares?

I enjoy Sundays more than I probably admit at the time. I suppose it is expected that I make the occasional grumble. But weekly pressures disappear when I am surrounded by Julie and the kids.

Sunday is a day for winding down, for relaxing. During the afternoon, Julie and I sit down and plan how we are going to furnish the rest of our new bungalow. (At that time we were still only partially moved in and I was sometimes forced to

139

spend midweek nights in a North London hotel while Julie and the girls stayed with Julie's family in East Grinstead.)

One of the girls decides to experiment with a box of matches and leaves a burn-mark in her bedroom carpet. So after Julie has had her say, I take the 'guilty party' into her room and explain to her the real dangers of playing with matches. Sometimes, being a dad means showing a serious, frowning face. And when the incident is as serious as this one was, that face has to do more than frown. You have to be logical rather than angry and loud. A few tears, a big hug and the whole business is forgotten.

Monday Julie gets the girls ready for school. Louise is still too young to go, but she misses her sisters when they leave in the morning, and Jasper plays a big part in bringing back her smile.

The drive to Arsenal's London Colney training ground takes me forty-five minutes. I whip through some of the small villages, missing the busy Bedford traffic, and join the M1 just past Kempston.

Now I am thinking about Saturday's match from a totally constructive point of view. Because we always begin the week with a team-meeting during which we discuss the weekend match. We won, and some of the lads feel they have a right to be pleased. But the manager does not agree. Rightly, he points to the fact that perhaps we could have made more of our early advantage. Points are raised, thrashed out and thrown around the dressing room. One of the lads decides to be flippant. The manager cuts across him before the mood catches on. Sometimes, tempers become heated and players flare up when confronted with one of their mistakes. But players do accept the fact that these discussions – if properly conducted – are valuable. They help us to get our game and our form into perspective.

If we all took a back seat and allowed the manager to say his piece, the atmosphere would always be one of calm and serenity. But I doubt if the manager would appreciate a lack of enthusiasm such as that, and certainly the players would

140

have to question their attitudes if they found they were unable to contribute to the discussion.

One of the lads says: 'But we won. Why all the fault-finding?' What he forgets is that our display, while good, was nowhere near perfection. What display ever is? But while the ultimate aim is to achieve perfection, and that aim is still to be achieved, there must be room and time for discussion.

After the team-chat, we file out to begin our regular Monday training, geared to get rid of weekend stiffness and aches. I feel a few twinges, but nothing to worry about. By now, I have been a professional for long enough to make that judgement.

One or two players visit the physiotherapist after training. The rest of us shower and change, then have lunch at the training ground. I have an afternoon appointment, so I politely decline invitations to have a few afternoon lagers.

I point my Lancia towards London and arrive - twenty minutes late - for an appointment with a promotions man who is convinced I will be interested, if not fascinated, in the proposition he has to offer. He wants me to devote time to his proposition - time I do not have. Because if I become involved with this man, it will overlap with my football career, and that is impossible. But no matter how hard I try, he refuses to understand my point of view.

Finally, I explain, in clipped sentences, that I must train to maintain my level of professional playing standards. And if I do not train, the level drops. And if the level drops, I am dropped. And if I am dropped, people such as the promotions man will not want to make me such propositions in the first place. Quite simple really. He is still staring at me as I head for the door.

I am anxious to get home because a man is coming to see me about installing an oil tank in the garage. Without it, our heating system is non-existent. My foot stamps down on the gas pedal and the Lancia heads for home.

The man is there when I arrive. Good old Julie. She has kept him occupied with cups of coffee and rural chat. Soon, I

141

am back in the domestic role, sleeves rolled up, arms covered in oil and dust.

After dinner I bath the girls, put them to bed – it's my turn – and resign myself to another 'walkies' session with Jasper. Fortunately, he enjoys one particular walk that just happens to encompass the pub down the road. Julie's eyebrows do a tango, and Jasper and I trudge up the lane, in the opposite direction, muttering darkly about wives with suspicious minds.

Tuesday This is graft day. We do not have a midweek match, so I know that I have to be prepared for a day of slog, sweat and hard work. Quick kisses from all the girls, a wag of Jasper's tail and I'm zooming down the M1, all the time getting my mind accustomed to the reality that today, pal, you are going to suffer.

We get changed – one or two lads are a bit late and get suitably corrected – and despite the customary moans and groans, we are professionals. The work gets done.

The manager and coach give us a real grilling. A warm-up, sprints, distance running, more sprints, exercises. We are too shattered to even protest when yet another demand is made of our aching bodies. For a fleeting moment, I consider giving that promotions man a call, but the thought sends shudders through the parts of my body which I can still feel, and I buckle down to work.

Every time I complete a run, I swear that I'm not going to be able to manage another. But I do. We all do. The manager and coach allow no slackening off. And there is always the competitive spirit that demands you finish faster than your team-mates. Then, of course, there is your natural motivation. You are a professional. This is your bread and butter. I always try and get things into perspective as soon as I feel a moan coming on.

Jeers and laughter from the lads snap me out of my pain-defying thoughts. Jimmy Rimmer is struggling, and getting slower with every run. Jim's no master-athlete, but nor is he a slouch. And today, he is gasping for breath and trailing badly. The hoots or derision grow louder and Jim begins to go red in the face and lose his patience. Only when we get into the changing room do we understand why Jim has struggled. The rain has pelted down all morning. And Jim spent a good deal of time plunging around in his goalmouth to keep out the shots raining in on him. His kit is pounds heavier than usual – because a fair slice of London Colney's ground surface is on it. Poor old Jim's been running with a mud-handicap.

A quick shower, a salad lunch, and we go out again, this time for an hour, working on practical tactics. We explore the possibilities of a few free-kick routines. 'Chippy' Brady leaves me open-mouthed by the way he bends and curls the ball with a flick of his left foot. Then we go over some of our regular moves, always seeking to improve our timing, our understanding as a team-unit.

Frank Stapleton is feeling a bit depressed. He is worried about his form. So I give him a gee-up and tell him he is the best thing since sliced bread. I point out his strengths and how they benefit the team. He lifts his head and begins to grin. Sometimes he comes on with the 'Jack the Lad' attitude, and I smack him back down to earth. He is going to be one hell of a player. But at this stage of his career he is not sure whether he likes me or hates me. That's the way to have it. When he is down, I attempt to lift him. When his head disappears into the clouds for a while, I bring him down again. He will find the correct level with years and experience.

Players who have been in the game for a while and have seen a bit of life should make a point of helping young players in their club. When Frank and I hit form, we are a handful for any defence. But I must look to his game as well as mine. I believe this is a responsibility, not a favour.

I do a bit of devious plotting on the way home. Julie waves as I pull into the garage. Her eyebrows arch as I do my 'bad-back' routine.

'Had a hell of a day, love,' I mutter … Silence!

'My back is giving me a bad time. The manager says I must rest it.' … Silence!

143

I suppose I was resigned to curtain-hanging anyway. We start to drill holes in the wall above the windows, then the drill snaps. I have been trying to drill through a solid girder. Eventually, after a trip into Bedford before the shops shut, I tackle the girder with stronger tools. This time, after much huffing and puffing, we have curtains.

Just one thing left to do ... insert the last, vital little screws. The screws! Where the hell are they? Julie and I search every room, every drawer. Then I spot one screw, then another. We follow the trail out to the garage where Jasper, attempting to flash a weak grin, allows the rest of the screws plus the paper box to tumble out of his mouth.

Julie and I spend the rest of the evening relaxing and chatting about the old days, when we lived in a terraced house. It is funny the way people forget the bad times and only remember the highspots, the fun, the laughs.

Wednesday   This is the life. Who would be anything other than a professional footballer? It's my day off. I stretch my legs, sit up to give the girls a kiss before they go to school and wave a threatening fist at Jasper as he slyly sneaks in behind the girls and attempts to take me by surprise.

I have planned the whole day. A walk with Jasper, a trip down to Bedford to have the car serviced, home for lunch, the afternoon wrapped up behind a good book, dinner followed by a few hours down at the pub with my new neighbours.

Oh, the dreams of mice and men! My sleep-in lasts ten minutes. The 'Hound of Radwell' manages to sneak in again and lands a paw firmly on my chin. Two licks are sufficient. I get up, muttering unprintable oaths about Crufts, kennels and muzzles.

Julie is up and very busy around the house, With three daughters – one of them always there demanding attention – it is impossible not to be busy. I look at Jasper and harken to the call from the kitchen that breakfast is ready. Jasper loses this round to an empty stomach.

I storm through breakfast, glancing through the papers as I chomp, and make a dash for the door before Julie can think of any chores to be done. I remind her, as I reach the door, that we have been told to make the most of our day off. She's heard that one before as well, and points to the garden. I send another of Jasper's rubber bones rocketing into the bottom corner of the oven with an effortless flick of the left foot. But Julie is still pointing towards the garden, grinning.

Even Jasper has that hang-dog look about him as I head out to unwrap the lawn-mower. Half an hour of graft on a garden that still resembles the Yorkshire Moors in January, and I decide it's time for a break. An exchange of glances with Jasper and he trots indoors to get his lead. But when I nip around the side of the garage, Julie has two shopping bags and the car keys at the ready. Even the dog loses his patience with me, drops the lead and walks away.

When we return from Bedford, we unpack another of the massive boxes crammed with our belongings. This is always enjoyable. It can be a shock to come across some of the old bits and bobs of yesteryear that have survived four or five family moves.

Then I collect Claire and Jeanette from school. I manage to persuade them that I have broken my leg and therefore cannot let them use me as a Maypole.

The two girls decide to have a game of draughts. I watch, much to their disgust, and cannot resist the temptation to correct mistakes. 'Oh Daddy, please!' snaps Claire. Jeanette snatches the opportunity to make a decisive move. I can sense a bit of antagonism building up and have to be careful to be seen to be fair to both players. If I so much as hint at helping one girl more than the other, war ensues.

Howls and hisses bring Julie and me racing out to the back. Jasper has made yet another unsuccessful attempt to introduce himself to the cat – and again been scratched across the nose. The girls forget all about their game and dash to the scene. I sense tears in the offing, so I make one responsible for the cat and the other for the dog. Peace settles on The New Bungalow for another night.

Thursday Usual morning routine sees me arrive at London

Colney just after 10.15. We begin training at 10.30. This is another long session, but not the slog of a Tuesday.

We begin with the warm-up then move on to doing skills under pressure by playing possession football. This is usually seven v seven without goals, in a five-a-side pitch area. We start steadily, then quickly switch to two-touch which increases the pressure and sharpens reactions. Players have to release the ball early to their team-mates.

This is not a session for those players who sometimes wake up three hours after getting up! You can be made to look a clumsy fool if you do not concentrate one hundred per cent. I bomb a few shots at Jimmy Rimmer, slicing some of them high and wide. Caustic comments from the wings serve to sharpen my accuracy. Then we move on to tactics and discussing Saturday's match. This is extra-special for me, and for Paddy Howard, because we play Newcastle United at Highbury!

Paddy and I chat about the match before the general discussion begins. We both resolve to treat this match just as we would any other. We have to. This is the professional level of thought.

Now we get down to business. We know, more or less, what their team will be. So we work on moves aimed at exploiting their weaknesses, and the weaknesses of some of their players. This is where Paddy and I do have a lot to contribute.

We finish our session in the small gym, doing five dozen sit-ups followed by a bath. Then it's soup, bangers, chips and beans in the canteen. A bottle of milk washes it all down. All thoughts are beginning to focus on 3p.m. Saturday. There is general chat, but our minds are adjusting to the routine, just as our bodies have adjusted to our physical routine all week.

I have a business appointment in London that afternoon. This time it is a session with a photographer. He is a good pro and the session takes no time at all. But now I have the rush-hour traffic to beat, and I want to collect the girls from school. I have to convince them that my 'broken leg' is mending slowly, very slowly.

146

The evening finds me in the pub, a few miles from home. Already I imagine those accusing thoughts. 'Out on the booze two days before a match?' No, not at all. I am there for a very worthy cause. I have been asked to smash a two-gallon-sized whisky bottle, filled with money. Once out of the bottle, the money goes on its way to a home for handicapped children. By now, of course, I am on the carbohydrate diet. So I have no qualms about eating a few sandwiches after dinner. And no doubt the bar of chocolate waiting for me in the car will also be gone before I get home. Otherwise it has to be shared with Jasper!

More thoughts about the Newcastle game. Julie and I talk about the friends we left behind in Geordie Land. I think back to that plot of land I bought, where I had planned to build our own house. Funny how things work out. There we are, in the very heart of the Bedfordshire countryside, miles from the north-east. Yet only a matter of months ago, we did not know where we would end up. Only that we were leaving Newcastle.

We chat, we sit in long but mutual and understood silences. All is quiet, except in my head.

Friday Friday training is light. We work at loosening and sharpening both body and mind. After the routine warm-ups, we gradually build up to sprinting pace. Some of the lads are showing the old and familiar signs of early tension. Match-day is around the corner – and it shows.

We move on to a five-a-side game so that we can all get a good feel of the ball. This is played at a furious pace, with the manager risking life and limb by joining in. We enjoy the five-a-side games, but also treat them very seriously. In effect they are our last chance of the week before we go out and play for real.

After lunch and a bath or shower, we collect our complimentary tickets. Our chat is about everything and anything but the match. This is the way with footballers. This is the routine, although sometimes it does not feel like a routine.

Home to relax. This time Julie, who is also wrapped up in

the routine, does everything bar bring me pipe and slippers. She knows that Friday is a day when I must be wound-down, yet mentally keyed up – sounds a bit Irish, but that's the way it is. A good carbohydrate dinner is followed by a night in front of the telly – after walking Jasper and conceding that my broken leg has healed and I can become a Maypole. It very much depends on how you view relaxation. For me, it's all about being at home, in the thick of things and miles away from work.

That is a week in the life of yours truly. Of course our dressing-room arguments are more detailed and 'colourful'. Of course there are disagreements at home and at work. But they are not what is important. What does matter is that you appreciate what I mean by the life that faces you, and the importance and value of your routine.

THIRTEEN
A Day in the Life

Breakfast in bed! It is wonderful to have three daughters. On the big day, life is a bowl of cherries. Well, maybe not quite cherries, but certainly a glass of orange juice, toast with thick marmalade (the carbohydrates again) and cups of tea (one in bed and one while I am in the bath).

Yes, it is match-day – the most important day of the professional footballer's week. On this very special day you focus all your week's work into ninety minutes of concentrated work.

On this particular Saturday morning I feel that tingle of magic running through my bones. I have always believed in just a little bit of magic, and for me that magic reserves its rare appearances for certain big days. Like my home debut for Newcastle against Liverpool when I scored a hat-trick in a 3-2 win. Like our FA Cup semi-final with Burnley when I scored both goals in a 2-0 win. Like the night we blitzed Cyprus 5-0 ...

This is not something that can be explained in logical terms. It is a feeling, an instinct, a belief in destiny that makes it difficult for me to stop grinning as I emerge from the bathroom and head for the more select end of the wardrobe. On with the shirt, collar and tie. Out with the best trousers and jacket. Arsenal are a club of great tradition, and the least that a professional footballer can do on matchday is look respectable. He may go out and play the worst ninety minutes of his life. But in terms of representing his club, he has not let them down before or after the match. This is very important. Never scoff at tradition. It is a very valuable backbone in this instance. More a case of personal pride and pride in your club.

Now I sneak out of the bedroom, peep around the corridor and tiptoe into the kitchen. At all costs I must avoid contact with Jasper, especially if he has spent most of the morning romping around the garden with the girls. His paws will leave rose patterns all over my clothes.

Julie is very quiet. She is longing to say something about today's game, but she knows that there is nothing worth saying until I get home. Then, perhaps, we shall have plenty to discuss.

Let nobody ever kid you that match-days are anything other than bad for the nervous system. The feeling is a mixture of that hollow sensation in the pit of the stomach and a longing to go out on the pitch and 'get on with it'.

Well, drumming my fingers on the table-top is not going to get me to Highbury, so I wink at Julie, she returns a large warm smile and the Lancia is nosing through countless little villages once again.

Plenty of time for thought in the car. I wonder what the Newcastle lads will say when we meet? Will Gordon Lee smile when I say hello, or will he twitch? I must congratulate Geoff Nulty on his in-depth newspaper articles. If my doctor knew as much about me as Geoff appears to think he knows, I would change doctors.

Without doubt, this is not just another match-day, much as I fight to tell myself that it is. What I must do is play my normal game, do my normal team job and avoid the temptation to upset the team rhythm through any personal motives.

I hold no grudges. Why should I? I loved most of my time at Newcastle. The fans were different class. I made some very good friends – on and off the pitch. Only the last few months were sour. But that is all water – some of it muddy – under Tyne Bridge.

Your playing career will undoubtedly encompass many match-days. Some will be extra-special days – days when you find yourself playing against professionals who were your constant companions for years. You must know how to cope with such an occasion. You must be bigger than the day itself and capable of making that day yours. It all boils down to being a human being – an individual, with feelings and emotions. Hiding those emotions and feelings from the public eye is one thing. But attempting to deny their existence, even to yourself, is foolish.

My transfer from Newcastle to Arsenal did not go through without a lot of ballyhoo. There were some unexpectedly hurtful things said, things that angered me more because of my feelings for Julie and the girls. No man enjoys seeing his daughters looking puzzled every time they read unpleasant articles in newspapers or hear caustic interviews on radio and television all about their dad.

But having said all that, you are a big boy now. You must behave like a man and not like an immature child. No vendetta, no nasty comments. In situations such as the one I face at Highbury today, you must be cool, calm, smiling and completely above all the fresh waves of ballyhoo.

Oh yes, the publicity goes on. All week, I have read countless and very varied articles concerning our match with Newcastle United. Some have been pointed, others downright comical. Reading some of the articles, the man in the street could be forgiven for coming to Highbury expecting to see knives, knuckle-dusters and massive banners smeared with hate messages.

Every minute the excitement grows. I have that feeling, I know this is going to be a good day, a magical day. When I was a boy I used to follow the exploits of Roy of the Rovers, the famous comic hero. Jokingly, I once told a journalist that I believed I was Roy of the Rovers. Needless to say, it stuck.

So I thought, why not? I know what Roy would do on a day such as today. The same thing I want to do. Don't be alarmed, I'm not cracking up. Just a little example of my personal, secret magic. It never hurt anyone, especially when you know very well that once you get out on the pitch, you have to make everything happen for you. The realism always comes last – just in time for the kick-off.

Before I realise it, the Lancia is bobbling down the stoned approach to South Herts Golf Club, Totteridge. This is where the Arsenal players meet for lunch before home games. The club provides post-lunch amusements such as a snooker table, colour television and the enigmatic Dai Rees, who I swear is a frustrated footballer who turned to golf. We complete our lunch and immediately switch on the football on television. By now I am well into a bar of chocolate.

After the football – and the usual sarcastic comments that greet every goal screened that is scored by anyone other than an Arsenal player – we have our final team-chat with the manager before leaving for the ground. The butterflies begin to tickle. We arrive at Highbury between 1.30 and 1.45 and some of the lads like to put on training kit and warm up for about twenty minutes in the gym. Not me. I prefer to relax and have a chat with the girls who serve in the players' lounge. Nothing like a natter over a cup of tea to dispel any lingering jitters.

Today, however, that cup of tea is hurried. Because I want to be at the main entrance when the opposition arrive. Now there is no doubt in my mind, and all attempts at pretence are a waste of time. Today is special. I just face up to that reality that always hits you last of all. It would be a pathetic lie to say that today is just another match-day. We are playing Newcastle United, and every moment of my day so far has been spent repeating that fact in my brain.

John Motson of BBC's 'Match of the Day' is there, discussing the format for the afternoon with his colleagues. I join the conversation, and inevitably it moves around to how I view my prospects against my former colleagues.

'As you played and trained with them for so long,' says John, 'don't you think they will know so much about you and your play that they will be able to counteract you?'

I reply that possibly that may be the case, but I am hoping that they regard me just as another member of the opposition and that they give equal regard to the rest of the Arsenal team. But if Newcastle give me any 'special treatment', such as denying me space throughout the match, they will create space for my team-mates. John frowns, then accepts the reply. I am not sure whether he accepts the point, but he accepts the reply.

Our conversation continues until the Newcastle United team coach arrives outside the main entrance. After a short wait, I see the first of the familiar faces coming through the doors. For one fleeting second, I wonder just where I am and what I am supposed to do or say. But that moment passes, as do a few thousand fleeting memories, and I wait to see who makes the gesture of saying hello.

Some of the lads come over for a brief chat. Others walk straight by without as much as a nod. A few weak, indecisive smiles here and there. Very much a case of 'follow my leader'. I suppress a smile.

To be honest, I was not too sure what to expect in the way of a greeting (or the lack of one) after the slanging matches that followed my transfer. The lads who did come up for a chat were the very lads I expected to make that gesture of friendship, which I appreciated. Sometimes you wonder how it is possible to go through so many experiences and so many emotions with a group of fellow human beings only to discover that there was little or nothing holding you together except the will to play and the will to win.

Do not live in a fools' paradise. You are in a profession. But just as newspapers are fish-and-chip paper by midnight, so are footballers has-beens and yesterday's news the moment their careers end. Somewhere in the middle of those extremes lies the extraordinary instant relationship that exists between footballers.

Today's team-mate, however, is tomorrow's opponent. So what do you do? How do you treat him? How do you react when he knocks you for six with a boot in the back? You pick yourself up and treat him the way you treat every other opponent. Only after the game do you worry about whose turn it is to buy the lagers.

Soon I am getting changed, doing my pre-match warm-up

153

exercises. One by one the Arsenal players come up to Paddy Howard and myself and wish us a great game each. And they really mean it. It is a strange thing in football that when a player faces his former team-mates, he wants his new colleagues to do well and to win. But his team-mates not only want to win, they want the player himself to be the star of the show. This is a sincere feeling and one which gives the player a hell of a morale boost before he goes out on the pitch. It is not a big thing, nor is it made into a big thing in the dressing-room. But it is the way each of your team-mates winks, gives you the thumbs up or makes a point of patting you on the back and saying: 'This is your day, pal, go out and stuff them.' That is music to the ears of any normal, emotional human being who longs for a word of support from the new as he prepares to face the old.

At 2.55 we leave the dressing-room and trot out on to the pitch. Paddy and I are understandably apprehensive about the greeting we are going to receive from the thousands of Geordies who have made the journey down for the match. They are massed at the 'clock end' and everyone is waiting for their reaction as we appear for the first time. Thank heavens they did not let Paddy or me down. In a nutshell, we were subjected to humorous abuse – exactly what we both expected, and we took it in the right spirit.

The Newcastle supporters are never lost for a word, and they give our legs a good pulling in the pre-match kickabout. I reply by giving them a wave. There is a moment's confusion before they combine their good-humoured catcalls with a warmer-than-expected blast of noise. So much for the much-publicised 'hate campaign'!

Now I take stock of the pitch, the weather and the whole atmosphere. The Arsenal fans are giving Paddy and me all the counter-support possible. The atmosphere is good. It is alive, keen and constant. Now it is up to us, the players, to do our stuff and stoke that atmosphere into a cauldron of emotion.

The attendance is over 34,000. They are no doubt generating the atmosphere to keep warm as well as out of natural

154

enthusiasm. The day is cold and biting, the pitch hard, slippery and dotted with patches of ice. Not an ideal day for frills.

A quick rub of the hands, a yell of encouragement all round, and the game gets under way. Immediately, the fans respond with a roar of approval. Newcastle are obviously not going to be caught by an early sucker-punch, and goalkeeper Mick Mahoney gets an early touch of the ball.

Already it is clear that defenders are going to struggle to turn on the surface, and indeed, we are all going to struggle to keep our balance in certain situations. The lottery ingredient is not to the players' liking, but it has the crowd in full voice. A few players end up on their bums, a few tackles go haywire and the ball pings around before some pattern is established. When it is, it's Newcastle who land the first, painful, blow. I can only watch as Micky Burns, the man Newcastle converted from winger to central striker when I left, gives Newcastle a very early lead. The Newcastle fans go wild. The Arsenal fans are stunned.

I look over to Paddy. He gives me one of his intense frowns and waves his fists in encouragement at the rest of the defence. This is a time for calm heads and absolutely no slagging off. We adopt the professional approach and play our way into a commanding position. We equalise, Newcastle are rocked back on their heels and I give us the lead, gleefully directing the ball into Newcastle's net at the North Bank End.

At half-time we troop off feeling ten feet tall. Newcastle are shattered. By now they are 3-1 down. Goals by Trevor Ross, Frank Stapleton and yours truly have partially silenced the Magpies' hordes of supporters. The pieces are slotting into place. I feel that tingle again. That magic is working. I know it is. But how can I pass on the message. So I don't bother trying. I just shake a fist and indicate that now is the time for finishing off the job.

Into the second half, attacking the clock-end where the Geordies are massed, I steal in to make it 4-1. Now we have Newcastle by the throat. Or do we? Suddenly, from a position of total mastery, we are slipping backwards. I can feel the tide changing. So can the fans. There is panic in the air as Newcastle pull back one goal then another through Alan Gowling and Micky Burns.

We rally, voices are raised. No way are we going to surrender a point in this game. Sleeves are rolled up - nobody out there feels the cold now, and if they do then they should have the decency to go off - and Newcastle's wave of pressure is stemmed just in time. Once again, the tide turns. A much nicer feeling.

Trevor Ross is wide on the right. He is dropping his head. He is going to lift over a deep cross. I make my run, two Newcastle defenders jump to challenge, but I can see the goal and the gap I want. My forehead punches that ball past Mick Mahoney. Highbury goes wild. I just lift both arms high in the air and walk back towards the middle.

A secret thought - Roy of the Rovers lives! But it is a very secret thought. Otherwise everyone will think I'm nuts.

Afterwards it's lemonade all round in a very happy and noisy Arsenal dressing-room. We all realise that Monday's routine team-chat will centre around the fact that we let in three goals. But who cares about Monday at this moment in time?

I sit in a corner, every last ounce of energy gone. I am suddenly very, very tired, mentally and physically. Thank God tomorrow is Sunday. Back come the waves of delight, the total appreciation of the moment. It is going to be difficult to be modest when I meet the press, though I am determined to try. But right now, I lean against the wall and let everything sink in. A hat-trick. Two points. A win. A week of hard work well rewarded. A job well done - and my own private dream come true.

I am not ego-tripping. I am providing you with an example which I want you to remember. If you work as hard as you know you can, and if you learn, as we all can, you will be able to make your dreams come true. And is that not what life - inside and outside football - is all about?

Stop rambling Macdonald. I am longing to do a jig, yet I

doubt if my legs will take the strain. I think of Julie's smile this morning. We'll crack a few bottles of champagne tonight. Paddy is just sitting in the bath, grinning and shaking his head. I know the feeling, pal. We just have different ways of experiencing it.

Emotions, emotions, emotions. God, it's bloody marvellous to be a professional footballer! There are so many emotions up ahead, waiting to hitch a ride with you on your road to success. Stop and pick them up. They will spark the magic in your life. Don't pass them by or ignore them. Feel them, live them. Otherwise your special days will just not be special.

I am always the last player to emerge after a match. I seem to take longer than anyone else to get changed and ready. But when I see the smiling faces of the pressmen, on this special day I simply smile back, a wide and lingering smile. They get the message. Enough said.

We have covered a fair few miles. I hope you have enjoyed the journey. Now, go out and *win*.